Mirko Knoll

Geostry

Mirko Knoll

Geostry

A Peer-to-Peer System for Location-based Information

Südwestdeutscher Verlag für Hochschulschriften

Impressum/Imprint (nur für Deutschland/ only for Germany)
Bibliografische Information der Deutschen Nationalbibliothek: Die Deutsche Nationalbibliothek verzeichnet diese Publikation in der Deutschen Nationalbibliografie; detaillierte bibliografische Daten sind im Internet über http://dnb.d-nb.de abrufbar.
 Alle in diesem Buch genannten Marken und Produktnamen unterliegen warenzeichen-, marken- oder patentrechtlichem Schutz bzw. sind Warenzeichen oder eingetragene Warenzeichen der jeweiligen Inhaber. Die Wiedergabe von Marken, Produktnamen, Gebrauchsnamen, Handelsnamen, Warenbezeichnungen u.s.w. in diesem Werk berechtigt auch ohne besondere Kennzeichnung nicht zu der Annahme, dass solche Namen im Sinne der Warenzeichen- und Markenschutzgesetzgebung als frei zu betrachten wären und daher von jedermann benutzt werden dürften.

Verlag: Südwestdeutscher Verlag für Hochschulschriften Aktiengesellschaft & Co. KG
Dudweiler Landstr. 99, 66123 Saarbrücken, Deutschland
Telefon +49 681 37 20 271-1, Telefax +49 681 37 20 271-0
Email: info@svh-verlag.de
Zugl.: Duisburg, Universität Duisburg-Essen, Dissertation, 2009

Herstellung in Deutschland:
Schaltungsdienst Lange o.H.G., Berlin
Books on Demand GmbH, Norderstedt
Reha GmbH, Saarbrücken
Amazon Distribution GmbH, Leipzig
ISBN: 978-3-8381-1138-4

Imprint (only for USA, GB)
Bibliographic information published by the Deutsche Nationalbibliothek: The Deutsche Nationalbibliothek lists this publication in the Deutsche Nationalbibliografie; detailed bibliographic data are available in the Internet at http://dnb.d-nb.de.
 Any brand names and product names mentioned in this book are subject to trademark, brand or patent protection and are trademarks or registered trademarks of their respective holders. The use of brand names, product names, common names, trade names, product descriptions etc. even without a particular marking in this works is in no way to be construed to mean that such names may be regarded as unrestricted in respect of trademark and brand protection legislation and could thus be used by anyone.

Publisher: Südwestdeutscher Verlag für Hochschulschriften Aktiengesellschaft & Co. KG
Dudweiler Landstr. 99, 66123 Saarbrücken, Germany
Phone +49 681 37 20 271-1, Fax +49 681 37 20 271-0
Email: info@svh-verlag.de

Printed in the U.S.A.
Printed in the U.K. by (see last page)
ISBN: 978-3-8381-1138-4

Copyright © 2010 by the author and Südwestdeutscher Verlag für Hochschulschriften Aktiengesellschaft & Co. KG and licensors
All rights reserved. Saarbrücken 2010

for my grandfather

Geostry

Abstract

An interesting development is summarized by the notion of "Ubiquitous Computing": In this area, miniature systems are integrated into everyday objects making these objects "smart" and able to communicate. Thereby, everyday objects can gather information about their state and their environment. By embedding this information into a model of the real world, which nowadays can be modeled very realistically using sophisticated 3D modeling techniques, it is possible to generate powerful digital world models. Not only can existing objects of the real world and their state be mapped into these world models, but additional information can be linked to these objects as well. The result is a symbiosis of the real world and digital information spaces.

In this book, we present a system that allows for an easy access to this information. In contrast to existing solutions our approach is not based on a server-client architecture. Geostry bases on a peer-to-peer system and thus incorporates all the advantages, such as self-organization, fairness (in terms of costs), scalability and many more. Setting up the network is realized through a decentralized bootstrapping protocol based on an existing Internet service to provide robustness and availability. To selectively find geographic-related information Geostry supports spatial queries. They - among other things - enable the user to search for information e.g. in a certain district only. Sometimes, a certain piece of information raises particular interest. To cope with the run on the single computer that provides this specific information, Geostry offers dynamic replication mechanisms. Thereby, the information is replicated for as long as the rush lasts. Thus, Geostry offers all aspects from setting up a network, providing access to geo-related information and replication methods to provide accessibility in times of high loads.

Acknowledgment

I would like to take the opportunity to thank everybody who aided and fostered the accomplishment of this book.

First of all, I would like to thank Prof. Dr.-Ing. Torben Weis, Dr. Arno Wacker, and Christian Becker for all the guidance and encouragement throughout my research period. Without the lively discussions with Arno I would have probably left university after graduating and would have never met Torben. Together they made my time at academia a very pleasant one and without their inspiration and support, I would never have completed this book on time.

My gratitude is extended to my colleagues and friends at the chair of Distributed Systems: my roommate Martin (thanks for the endless coding sessions), Kerstin, Henner, the Sebastians, and Matthias. All accompanied me throughout the long and winding journey until the completion of this book. Thanks to Bernd and Marianne for organizing everything I needed. Special thanks go to my colleagues from the University of Stuttgart, who gave me a wonderful start into my research time: Tobias, Nazario, Martina, Gregor and Frank.

There are also a number of people outside the department, whose collaboration enriched this work: To Carlos Furuti, who provided me with tons of valuable information about map projections; and to Ralph of the University of Stuttgart, who helped me through Mathematica and Maple conversion problems.

Last but not least, I am deeply grateful to my family and my friends. They gave me the much needed loving care and emotional support, shared their inspiring experiences and were always there for me.

Mirko Knoll
Duisburg, October 2009

Contents

Abstract   iii

Acknowledgment   v

1 Introduction   1
   1.1 The Geostry Idea 2
       1.1.1 Bootstrapping in Peer-to-Peer Systems 3
       1.1.2 Location-based Systems 5
       1.1.3 Replication 6
   1.2 Contributions 7
   1.3 Organization 8

2 Foundations   11
   2.1 Peer-to-Peer Systems 11
       2.1.1 Classification by Properties 14
       2.1.2 Classification by Generation 15
   2.2 Pastry - A Basis for Geostry 20
       2.2.1 Peer Setup 20
       2.2.2 Routing 23
       2.2.3 Peer Operation 24
   2.3 Bootstrapping in Decentralized Systems 26
   2.4 Location-based Services 27
       2.4.1 Location Modeling 28
       2.4.2 Spatial Queries 33
   2.5 Linearization 34
       2.5.1 Space-filling Curves 35
       2.5.2 Lindenmayer Systems 36
   2.6 Map Projections 38
       2.6.1 Basic Definitions 38

	2.6.2	Map Properties	41
	2.6.3	Projection Groups	46
	2.6.4	Summary	49
2.7	Replication		49

3 Bootstrapping in Peer-to-Peer Systems   55

3.1	System Model		55
3.2	Requirements		56
3.3	Design Rationale		56
3.4	Dynamic DNS		58
	3.4.1	Overview	58
	3.4.2	Bootstrapping	61
	3.4.3	Maintenance	62
3.5	Internet Relay Chat		64
	3.5.1	Bootstrapping Phase	65
	3.5.2	Joining the Overlay	66
	3.5.3	At Runtime	67
	3.5.4	Leaving	67
3.6	Evaluation		68
	3.6.1	DDNS	69
	3.6.2	IRC	70
	3.6.3	Open Issues	71
3.7	Summary		73

4 Spatial Queries   75

4.1	Location-based P2P & Locality		75
4.2	World Partitioning		76
4.3	Space-Filling Curves		80
	4.3.1	S-shaped Curve	81
	4.3.2	Lebesgue	81
	4.3.3	Peano	81
	4.3.4	Hilbert	82
	4.3.5	Fass II	83
4.4	Evaluation		83
	4.4.1	Mean Error Rate	84
	4.4.2	Small-World Populations	85
4.5	Position Queries		88

4.6	Region Queries	90
4.7	Neighborhood Queries	93
4.8	Summary	95

5 Replication 99
5.1	Introduction	99
5.2	Replication Goals & Challenges	101
5.3	System Model	102
5.4	Replication Design	103
	5.4.1 State 1: Direct object access	103
	5.4.2 State 2: Leafset Redirection	105
	5.4.3 State 3: Timeout - Deterministic Alternatives	105
	5.4.4 Replication Clean-Up	107
	5.4.5 Fast Converging Routes	108
5.5	Evaluation	109
	5.5.1 Scenarios	110
	5.5.2 Results and Analysis	110
5.6	Summary	112

6 Related Work 115
6.1	P2P-based location service	115
	6.1.1 P2P Systems: CAN	115
	6.1.2 Data Storage: OceanStore	116
	6.1.3 Data Distribution	116
6.2	Bootstrapping	118
	6.2.1 Peer-based approaches	118
	6.2.2 Mediator-based approaches	120
6.3	Spatial Queries	123
	6.3.1 Globase.KOM	123
	6.3.2 Schmidt's Approach	123
	6.3.3 Wierum's Approach	124
	6.3.4 Palma Project	124
	6.3.5 Distributed Space Partitioning Trees	124
6.4	Replication	125
	6.4.1 Passive Replication	125
	6.4.2 Cache-based Replication	125
	6.4.3 Active Content Replication	126

	6.4.4 OceanStore's Replica Management	126
	6.4.5 PAST's Initial Factor Assignment	127
	6.4.6 Static Replication Schemes	127

7 Conclusion   **129**

A Peirce Projection   **133**
   A.1 Projecting Geographical Coordinates 133
       A.1.1 Solving the Equations 134
   A.2 Calculating the Index on the Hilbert Curve 134

Glossary   **137**

Bibliography   **139**

List of Acronyms and Symbols   **151**

List of Publications and Contributions to Conferences   **153**

Index   **157**

List of Figures

1.1	Area of Research	2
1.2	The Geostry Process	3
2.1	First approach to peer-to-peer technology	16
2.2	Example for a pure peer-to-peer network	17
2.3	The super-peer concept	18
2.4	Use of distributed hash tables in P2P networks	19
2.5	State of a Pastry node	22
2.6	Routing a message in Pastry	22
2.7	The location service architecture	28
2.8	Cartesian coordinate system	30
2.9	Symbolic Models	31
2.10	Hybrid Model	32
2.11	Map of Stuttgart, Germany	33
2.12	Latitude and longitude	40
2.13	Illustration of common projections	42
2.14	Distances in a cylindrical map	43
2.15	Illustration of loxodromes	43
2.16	Distortions of equal-area projections	44
2.17	Equatorial Mollweide Projection	45
2.18	Mercator map showing a geodesic and a loxodrome	45
2.19	Tissot Indicatrices	47
3.1	Evaluations on DDNS	72
3.2	Evaluations on IRC	73
4.1	Mapping 2-dimensional coordinates on a 1-dimensional ring	77
4.2	2D World Model	79
4.3	Trivial S-shaped Curve	81
4.4	Lebesgue Curve (Order 1-3)	82

4.5	Peano Curve (Order 1-3)	82
4.6	Hilbert Curve (Order 1-3)	83
4.7	Fass II Curve (Order 1-3)	83
4.8	Mean Error Distribution of Space-Filling Curves	85
4.9	Generating small-world-like populations	86
4.10	Linear Population Rate	87
4.11	Error per Hotspot with dense and sparse populations	88
4.12	The requesting region intersects the curve twice	90
4.13	The elements of the Hilbert curve and the according prefixes	91
4.14	The DFA for generating the Hilbert Index	92
4.15	Approximating a neighborhood query through multiple region queries	95
4.16	The Hilbert curve in 3D	96
5.1	Illustration of Geostry's replication behavior	104
5.2	Fast Converging Routes	109
5.3	Accumulated Replication Simulation Results	111
5.4	Replication Simulation showing Load Distribution	113
A.1	The progression of the elliptic integral of the first kind	135

List of Tables

2.1	Definitions for Pastry routing algorithm	23
2.2	Samples of Lindenmayer Systems	39
2.3	Overview of Projections	50
2.4	Overview of popular Projections	51
3.1	Basic procedures used in the DDNS approach	60
3.2	Basic procedures used in the IRC approach	65
4.1	Mean Error Rate for each curve	84
4.2	Basic procedures used for implementing position queries	89
4.3	Basic procedures used for implementing region queries	94
5.1	Basic procedures during replication	103

List of Algorithms

1	Pseudo code for Pastry's routing algorithm	23
2	The main DDNS bootstrapping procedure	61
3	Checking whether to become a guardian	62
4	Checking the bootstrap peer	63
5	Checking the number of active guardians	63
6	IRC Bootstrapping in general	66
7	Self-Healing Mechanisms in the IRC	67
8	Pseudo code for calculating Hilbert Index for a POI	89
9	Supporting Region Queries	94
10	Check whether to start Leafset Replication	105
11	Check whether to start Hash Replication	106
12	Calculate Hilbert Index	135
13	HilbertIndex: Main Loop	136

Chapter 1

Introduction

Advances in sensor technology enable us to track the position of people outdoors and in-house. Using small sensor boards, we can gather a multitude of additional information about our environment. Furthermore, RFID tags allow us to track objects ranging from books to freight containers. The data gathered by such sensor systems is the basis for a digital world model. In home-automation scenarios these world models are not very huge and can easily be handled by commercial-off-the-shelf SQL databases. However, large-scale world models require an appropriate infrastructure. Until recently, vast server farms had to be established to provide large-scale context-information. Along with the costs for the servers, further costs for bandwidth, disk storage, and administration arise.

In contrast to the WWW, world models are highly dynamic, especially when they store the position of people and physical objects. Routing all of this dynamic data to a central server is not feasible. Therefore, we must try to store such dynamic data close to the location where it originates. Thus, a large-scale context service is ideally assembled of a set of tiny servers distributed across the globe and connected by high-bandwidth networks.

Although technically possible, such a large-scale infrastructure requires a significant investment. Especially projects that do not have a commercial backing cannot afford such an expensive infrastructure. Because of these drawbacks we are working on a P2P-based solution to get rid of an expensive fixed infrastructure for hosting context-based data. The idea is that those users and institutions who want to participate in a context-based application have to provide their share of bandwidth, CPU, and disk space. In doing so, everyone can contribute to and benefit from the system at virtually no cost. The resulting area of research is depicted in Figure 1.1.

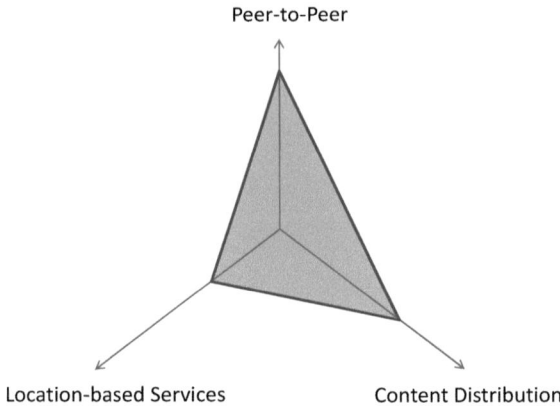

Figure 1.1: Area of Research

First, we address the fundamental problem of setting up a peer-to-peer system. Then we show, how to search for location-based information in this system and explain the replication mechanisms allowing data to be simultaneously requested by a larger amount of participants.

1.1 The Geostry Idea

Referring to Figure 1.2 every project starts with an initial idea. In contrast to a classic heavyweight server-based infrastructure, a single individual can create a location-based service (LBS) using peer-to-peer technology. To provide location-based data we assume each peer to use some kind of positioning technology, be it through the Global Positioning System (GPS), wireless triangulation or others. Starting a new P2P service however becomes a major problem. As there is no fixed infrastructure, it becomes difficult for other peers to find the newly established network.

This problem is generally known as the *bootstrapping* problem. When the first few participants are online, we can begin searching for information. Yet this raises the question how we actually search for location-based information in a peer-to-peer system. Usually, in such an LBS infrastructure there are services that organize the data in a special way, such that *spatial queries* like "what is the temperature in

1.1 The Geostry Idea

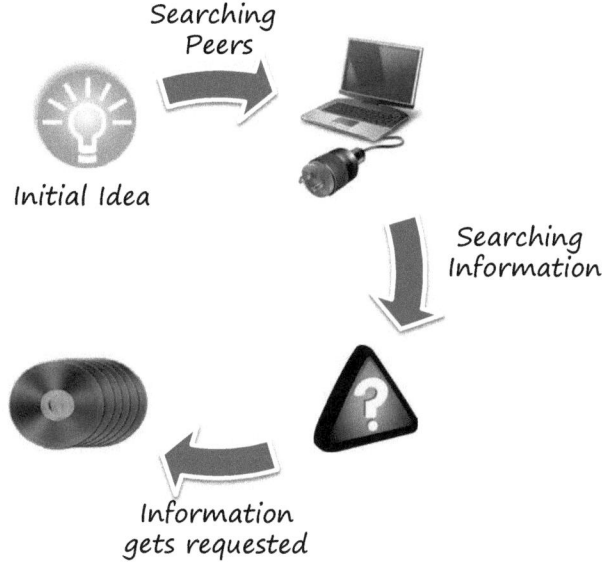

Figure 1.2: The Geostry Process

Berlin" can be easily answered. In P2P systems, peers have to provide a distributed service to allow for such queries. Imagine, our LBS grows in user numbers and more and more interesting data becomes available. At one point, a single peer will not be able to answer all incoming queries any more as there are too many peers interested in a specific data element. Therefore, in this case this specific data has to be *replicated* to other peers to guarantee availability even in the event of flash-crowds (here: a sudden increase of interest leading to a large group of interested parties).

1.1.1 Bootstrapping in Peer-to-Peer Systems

Over the last few years there has been excessive research on the area of peer-to-peer systems. New algorithms for message routing, storing or retrieving information etc. have been developed and improved. However, one essential aspect has been neglected in almost all of those works: the bootstrapping process. When a peer wants to join an existing P2P system, it has to contact at least one member of the P2P system to receive a list of further participants and begin communications. Initially, a peer is not aware of any recent peers in the network. The bootstrapping process therefore ensures that a peer is able to find other members of the P2P system it wants to join. This emphasizes the importance of a bootstrapping protocol as without it no communication will take place.

It is clear that in existing P2P systems like Bittorrent [1], eMule [2] or Gnutella [3] the problem had to be solved somehow. In fact, these systems make use of so-called well-known entry points. Newly arriving peers contact these points to retrieve information about other current users. The existing approaches however suffer from one of the following drawbacks:

- The well-known entry point poses a single point of failure (SPOF)
- The bootstrapping process requires some manual interaction

Though 53% of all Internet traffic is generated through Bittorrent (see Cachelogic [4]) - making it one of the most used services on the Internet - it becomes useless in the absence of the tracker. The tracker is responsible for maintaining a list of peers sharing the same file. A peer willing to download a file contacts the responsible tracker to receive this list. It then contacts the peers from the list and commences the download. Yet, when the tracker is gone, there is no chance to receive a list any more and thus downloads are rendered impossible.

In the area of file-sharing other services have become popular, e.g. Kazaa [5] and eDonkey [6]. Those services solve the bootstrapping by having the user download a special file. This file contains a list of peers which have been online recently. The peer then contacts peers from the list to join the peer-to-peer network. As the peer's average retention time in the P2P network is rather short, the list files get outdated soon. Therefore, recurring users often have to download these files before joining the overlay.

The protocol presented in this book runs on all nodes eliminating the single point of failure. Furthermore, it offers an automatic bootstrapping process overcoming the need for manual interaction during runtime, thus overcoming the drawbacks mentioned above.

1.1.2 Location-based Systems

The main objective of location-based services (e.g. Nexus Center of Excellence [7], Cooltown [8], Georgia Tech Home [9]) is the definition and realization of world models. In this scope, issues concerning communication, information management, methods for model representation and sensor data integration are covered. World models are then integrated into sample applications to derive basic requirements and evaluate system concepts. Besides the technical problems which result from merging different research areas from the fields of computer science, geographic information systems, and other technical fields, issues in the area of information security and social acceptability have been investigated.

In location-based services the collected information is processed and aggregated in so-called *context-servers*. These servers then provide user access to the data. However, hosting data always requires a certain infrastructure. Context-servers need to be deployed and this requires some preparatory work. This work includes hardware investments, bandwidth and management efforts that may easily become very costly. Therefore, until today these platforms are suited for either official institutions offering public services (e.g. navigation, opening hours of public buildings, etc.) or commercial providers (e.g. café, shop owners etc.). For private users it is unaffordable to put their data on context servers, as this would implicate further costs for hosting and manpower for coping with the management efforts. Both of these requirements pose an overkill to smaller projects.

By using a P2P overlay network we can get rid of an expensive fixed infrastructure. P2P systems are self-organizing and decentralized. This allows us to reduce the cost of ownership to a minimum as the costs for the resources (e.g. disk space, CPU power, bandwidth) are split between all peers [10, 11].

First solutions to P2P-based approaches providing an efficient one-dimensional lookup were presented in [12, 13]. Soon these approaches were extended to meet multi-dimensional lookups. [12] performs two-dimensional geographical range queries by applying a Z-curve linearization of the 2D space. However, this approach suffers from not matching the geographical distance with the numerical distance in the P2P node ID space. This results in inefficient query replies adding an additional delay [14]. The search for spatial content became the focus of [14–16]. However, these approaches apply a recursive division of the 2D space to assign designated zones to the available nodes. In case of high node fluctuation, the remaining nodes have to re-arrange the internal tree-structure to match the new situation. This results in the new zone layout and the respective messages to inform the participating nodes about the areas they are responsible for.

In summary, we present a novel architecture overcoming the storage problem. This architecture uses a flat hierarchy and a static zone model. Thereby we keep the management costs low whilst still allowing users to query for location-based data on a peer-to-peer basis.

1.1.3 Replication

As distributed systems grow, they tend to become consistently less reliable since more and more services - running on different computers - become vital to their function [17]. One way to combat this problem is to replicate the vital services and data to a multitude of other systems, such that the failure of a single system has no effect on the overall functionality. Therefore, replication techniques belong to the oldest and most important topics in the area of distributed systems. The first algorithms and concepts thus have already been developed in the early 80s.

A first form of replication occurs when nodes request and copy data from one another. This form of interim saving is called "passive replication" and comes at no additional cost. An extension of this scheme is used by [18, 19]. As content passes through the nodes in the network, peers cache the files to increase the availability. Therefore, this scheme is called "cache-based replication". Later approaches tried to decrease the amount of files to be replicated and used different methods to decide which data to replicate and how often [20–22]. However, these approaches are not suitable for location-based systems as they do not take location into account. Thus, information for a certain location may be replicated to places where there is no interest for this information, e.g. information about Stuttgart is replicated to Tokyo.

In this book, we present an efficient and dynamic replication scheme replicating data according to its position. To further improve the availability additional copies will be placed at well-known positions in the peer-to-peer network.

1.2 Contributions

In this book we present a suite of algorithms to provide a location-based service based on peer-to-peer technology. These algorithms are suitable for stationary devices like desktop computers or sensors. Using the location as a key in peer-to-peer systems, participants are able to retrieve the most accurate information available at a certain time.

More specifically, the main contributions of this book are as follows:

- We derive and analyze the requirements for setting up a peer-to-peer network in absence of a central authority.

- We develop a novel bootstrapping scheme using existing Internet services. These services are widespread and heavily distributed. Therefore, some services (e.g. DynDNS by Dynamic Network Services, Inc.) achieve an uptime of 100% [23]. This "guarantees" a successful bootstrap at any time.

- We extend the bootstrapping scheme to offer resilience against multiple simultaneous node failures.

- In Chapter 4 we present a novel solution to create a location-based service using peer-to-peer technology. Thereby, all costs and maintenance works are fairly spread on all participants further eliminating the single point of failure.

- We analyze the ideal assignment of node identifiers, such that we achieve optimal locality. To simulate a realistic peer distribution we use a small-world distribution as underlying scenario.

- In Section 4.4 we derive the optimal solution to the locality problem by using space-filling curves for the given scenario.

- Using the results from the preceding sections, we demonstrate how we can implement spatial queries in our peer-to-peer system in Section 4.5.

- We analyze the requirements for an efficient replication scheme for peer-to-peer networks in Section 5.2.

- In Section 5.4 we present algorithms for an efficient replication scheme able to handle highly dynamic data.

- We enhance this scheme to offer a high uptime and provide resilience in the event of flash-crowds. This is achieved by replicating highly requested data to peers in the immediate vicinity of the source and at well-known locations.

- Including the location of data in our replication scheme, we are able to store and replicate information in the near surroundings of their origin. This makes sure that the data is available at the location(s) it is most likely to be requested.

We complement these contributions with a detailed performance evaluation of our algorithms.

1.3 Organization

The central focus of this book lies on the design and evaluation of a distributed location-based service. In addition we explore in which ways Geostry can be extended to meet diverse goals ranging from the initial setup of a peer-to-peer system to the replication of data. Accordingly, the remainder of the book is structured as follows:

Chapter 2: Foundations

This chapter introduces the technologies used in this book. We thereby give an overview of existing peer-to-peer technologies and an insight into location modeling. Thereby we give different possibilities for determining object locations and the spatial queries to ask for those objects. The chapter then closes with a short introduction into the field of replication technologies.

Chapter 3: Bootstrapping in Peer-to-Peer Systems

In this chapter we motivate the necessity for an effective and efficient bootstrapping protocol. To the best of our knowledge we are the first to present such a protocol. We thereby used two existing Internet services, namely the Distributed Dynamic Name Service (DDNS) (see Section 3.4) and the Internet Relay Chat (IRC) (see Section 3.5). Our evaluation in Section 3.6 shows, that we fulfilled all requirements mentioned in Section 3.2.

Chapter 4: Spatial Queries

After showing how Geostry does its bootstrapping, we then explain how we integrate a location-based system in a peer-to-peer system. Therefore, we map Earth to a 2-dimensional map and use a space-filling curve for the final dimension reduction. The resulting index of the space-filling curve then serves as a node's ID. In the following, we show how the various types of spatial queries can be implemented in our system.

Chapter 5: Replication

This chapter encourages the need for replication of data in a peer-to-peer network in Section 5.2. Sudden bursts of interest in a specific data element lead to a high load on a single peer. To counter this amount of requests we propose a new replication protocol as shown in Section 5.4. The experimental measurements in Section 5.5 prove the efficiency of our protocol.

Chapter 6: Related Work

There have been ideas to solve the above mentioned problems earlier. In this chapter, we present the major approaches in the field of location-based services, bootstrapping protocols and replication techniques. These works presented in Chapter 6 however differ from our approach and/or cannot be used effectively in our scenario.

Chapter 7: Conclusion

In the final chapter, we conclude this book with the most important findings and give an outlook on interesting future work areas.

Chapter 2

Foundations

In this chapter, we give a detailed overview of all the technologies that are used in Geostry. We begin with an introduction to peer-to-peer systems, the "successor" to traditional client-server systems. Thereafter, we take a more precise look at Pastry, as it is the framework on which Geostry bases. In contrast to client-server systems, in peer-to-peer systems usually there does not exist a centralized entry point. Therefore, participating peers need a special protocol - called bootstrapping - to find other peers. After explaining the basic bootstrapping protocol, we illustrate the use of location-based services, including the modeling of location and spatial queries. Then we explain the mathematical background for space-filling curves and their application in our peer-to-peer system. This simplifies the understanding of Geostry's architecture. We conclude this chapter with a brief overview of map projections and the replication of data.

2.1 Peer-to-Peer Systems

Peer-to-peer systems have become a key technology over the last few years. For some - e.g. Andy Oram - peer-to-peer is even "fundamental to the architecture of the Internet" [24]. However, it is difficult to find *one* definition for peer-to-peer systems. Most people use the term to address communication between equals, which in our scenario relates to the communication between computers in a network. As all members are equal, they are not bound to a certain role. During their participation in the network, they can call on foreign services as well as provide their own service for others. Thus, in some cases peers may act as servers whereas in other cases they act as clients. Peers are therefore sometimes called "servant" [25].

One of the key components of a peer-to-peer architecture is the *overlay network*. The overlay network puts a new logical view of its participants on top of the physical network. Thus, peers may be direct neighbors in the overlay network though they are multiple hops apart. The newly generated topology allows for a creation of alternative routes and further enables the peers to use common functions like Lookup or Search. Using the lookup operation, peers may identify the corresponding peer being responsible for a distinct object (Object-ID). Lookups are used in structured overlays and with the search operation, peers are able to search for objects matching certain criteria (e.g. filename). Whereas in structured overlays lookups are used (see Section 2.1.1) to identify "the peer" responsible for a certain object, search operations are used in unstructured overlays to find at least one match. As soon as a peer with the desired object has been found, the data transfer between the peers starts.

Recently, more and more application developers move from a traditional client-server structure to the more advanced P2P-based structure. This is mostly due to the many advantages that come along when using peer-to-peer technology. Some of the most important advantages are:

Self-organizing

A data center, which is needed to deploy an application for a huge amount of users, needs technicians for the maintenance and consumes a lot of electricity. This results in high costs for the operator, which in turn are passed to users. A P2P system offers the ability to organize the workload on all participating members. Thereby, no central server farm or computing center is needed, eliminating the costs for the operator.

Decentralized

A decentralized network supports the self-organizing abilities. By providing algorithms that can run on many peers simultaneously, the need for a central server farm is eliminated. Work loads are distributed and processed on all peers in the network. Thereby the load for each peer remains low, but the overall performance surpasses even high-end supercomputer. For example, the Seti@home Project with all its users achieves 15 TeraFLOPS, whereas IBM's ASCI White is rated at 12 TeraFLOPS [26]. However, the most important feature is the increased robustness.

Whereas an application in a server-client scenario will become unavailable in case of a server error (single point of failure) the decentralized application is not necessarily effected by the error of a single peer. Resources may be reduced, yet the overall functionality remains available.

Cost-sharing

Another advantage goes with the decentralization. Using a centralized computer center involves a lot of costs for building, maintaining and running. The decentralization spreads the costs for resources (file storage, CPU power, energy consumption, etc.) over all peers. Using the Seti@home Project as a reference again, we can see that the project has already consumed $500K. However, IBM's ASCI White costs around $110 million [26].

Scalable

A centralized computing center is designed to serve a specified amount of users. In case the service provider cannot attract enough users, the system is underemployed and therefore not cost-efficient. In the other case, the system has more users than it can serve. Then, the overall performance per user degrades and the computing center becomes the bottleneck. Summarized, resources are dropping the more users the service has. In peer-to-peer systems this is different. The more participants the network has, the more resources are available for everybody, as each user adds a little bit of its computing power, file storage etc. to the system. Therefore, peer-to-peer systems are superior in comparison to client-server systems when it comes to scalability.

Dynamic

Peer-to-peer systems are able to act dynamically to the situation in the network. Usually, peers join and leave a system continuously. The task management needs to adapt to this behavior. Work packages issued to a certain peer which are not finished within a certain timespan may be re-issued to another peer. Thereby, the system can cope with spontaneous node failures and departures and still run efficiently.

Increased Autonomy

In a client-server network, most if not all data is stored on the server. This makes it easy for the system operator to access this data or even alter it. In some countries, even government agencies apply a censorship for unpopular content and simply remove this data [27]. In P2P systems, each participant is autonomous. Therefore, the system cannot simply be shut down or regulated through a system administrator.

Anonymity

Recently, more and more Internet users have begun to realize how much private data has been collected about them. Huge service providers (e.g. Google [28]) are tracing and analyzing their users actions to build a user profile. This is done easily, as all computations are executed on centralized servers. Peer-to-peer systems make it more difficult to trace a single user. One user is only connected to a few other users while those are connected to others. Thereby, no one knows all participating members nor the actions they take. Meanwhile, there exist specialized P2P projects like Freenet [29]. Those are optimized for anonymity such that even the direct neighbors are not aware of a node's actions.

As there is not one definition for P2P systems covering all aspects, we subsequently give two orthogonal classifications. First, we follow the scheme of Hauswirth and Dustdar [11] and classify the P2P systems by their properties. Second, we explain the development of the various systems through the generation model.

2.1.1 Classification by Properties

The degree of *structure* divides P2P systems into two groups: structured and unstructured ones. In an unstructured P2P system (e.g. Gnutella [30]) peers do not have any knowledge about the information stored at other peers. Thus, a peer which cannot answer an incoming query has to forward the query to all of its neighbors, except for the one peer the query was initially received from. As this flooding causes severe traffic on the network, queries have to be limited in their range. After reaching a certain threshold (in Gnutella a time-to-live (TTL) of seven was used), queries simply will be dropped, even if no match has been found yet. In contrast, peers in a structured P2P system use indexes to maintain knowledge of the information

2.1 Peer-to-Peer Systems

their fellow peers offer. Furthermore, those peers keep a routing table to efficiently deliver messages. Therefore, peers can forward incoming queries in the direction of the peer which is most likely to have the desired information.

The degree of *hierarchy* is an important factor, when it comes to the assignment of tasks. In a P2P system with a flat hierarchy all peers share the same tasks. In a hierarchical P2P system, we differentiate peers in regard to their role. For instance in FastTrack [31] (Kazaa's search engine) there are regular peers and super-peers. Those super-peers offer different functionality (in this case: searches) than the regular peers do.

The degree of *coupling* gives detail about the level of integration. In a tightly coupled network there exists only one group of peers. In this group, all peers are assigned a designated role upon joining, e.g. for which information the peer is responsible or how messages should be treated. However, this mechanism limits the evolution of several independent networks existing side-by-side. In Gnutella or other loosely coupled systems, several networks may evolve separately, unite to a single network later on, or split up again.

2.1.2 Classification by Generation

In the following we give an orthogonal classification for an easier understanding of the evolution for P2P systems. This classification follows the style of Steinmetz's generation model [32].

1st Generation

One of the most popular representatives for a first generation peer-to-peer system is Napster [33]. Napster uses a central architecture with a server-client structure. That is, Napster provides one server (though in reality this is a server farm), which offers an index of all files available for sharing. However, no file is actually stored at those servers, they solely maintain IP addresses of the peers hosting the files. Fig. 2.1 illustrates the functionality of a first generation system. When peer A wants to download a file, it sends a query to the server and receives a list of potential providers. The peer then directly downloads the file from the remote peer (here: B), not needing the server any more.

As we can see, the server poses the bottleneck of the system. The more clients connect to the server, the less bandwidth there is for a single user. Regardless the bad scalability, the server also is a single point of failure. Without it, there is no exchange of shared files and therefore no peer knows where to download a desired file.

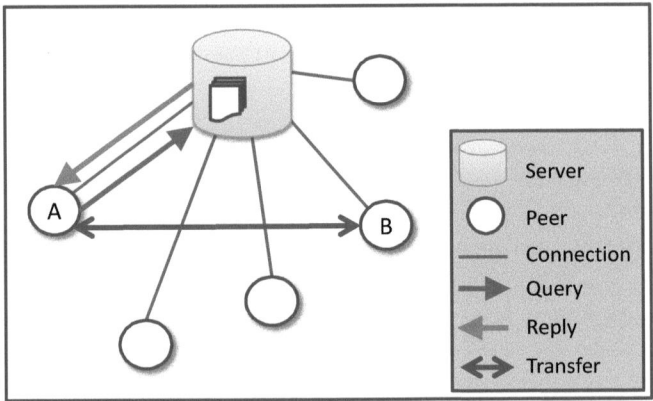

Figure 2.1: First approach to peer-to-peer technology

2nd Generation

The second generation tries to overcome the disadvantages of Napster and its siblings. Over time, two different approaches for achieving this goal have evolved: *pure* and *hybrid* systems.

Pure P2P systems, such as Gnutella, treat all peers equally. There is no central server as all peers act as server and client, thus becoming so-called servlets. To become aware of other active peers, they broadcast `Ping` messages. Peers receiving these messages store the address of the remote peer and answer with a `Pong`. As there is no index or server, the peer has no other chance than sending a query to all its neighbors (in Gnutella around 3-4). In case these nodes have the requested file, they reply with a `QueryHit` message. Otherwise, they decrement the TTL and forward the message to all of their neighbors until the TTL reaches zero.

Through the autonomy of peers a central server becomes obsolete. To download data, the peer floods the network with its query and eventually (if the query has not

2.1 Peer-to-Peer Systems

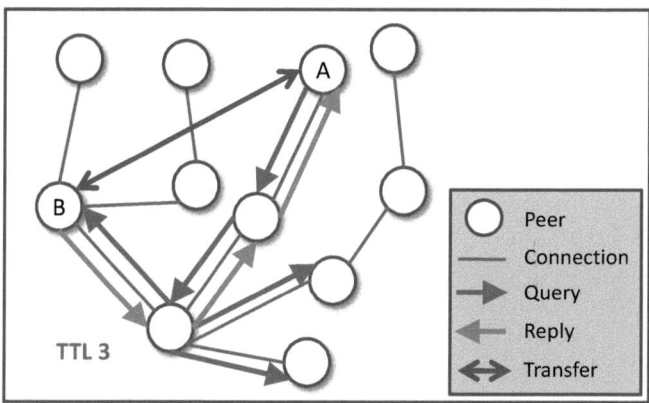

Figure 2.2: Example for a pure peer-to-peer network

timed out before a hit) receives the file. However, this flooding and the ping/pong mechanism for keeping the network view up-to-date massively stress the network. In fact, in dense networks packets collide so often that messages only make it to the third hop, even more reducing the probability of getting the desired file.

Hybrid P2P systems tried to get the best out of both yet known worlds: having an index for all available files (1st generation) and distributing the load on all peers (pure P2P networking). To do so, hybrid systems introduce a role model. High-performance peers with a fast CPU and Internet connection eventually become a super-peer. These super-peers serve as centralized entry points and maintain lists of other super-peers. Furthermore, they store information about the resources being offered by their peers. Clients download a server list from the Internet or use the one that comes with the client software. Once the client has connected to an active super-peer it becomes a peer on its part. As super-peers are interconnected among each other, the network structure results in a small-world-like pattern. For a file search, a peer sends its query to its super-peer. In case the super-peer does not have a peer with the desired file, it forwards the query to other super-peers (see Fig. 2.3). Eventually, A's super-peer receives a `QueryHit` from B's super-peer and sends it back to A. Upon this message, A may download the requested file from B.

This approach has improved scalability compared with a centralized approach or a pure P2P system. More powerful clients take the role of an index server and act as entry point for new clients. The success rate may not be as high as in e.g. in

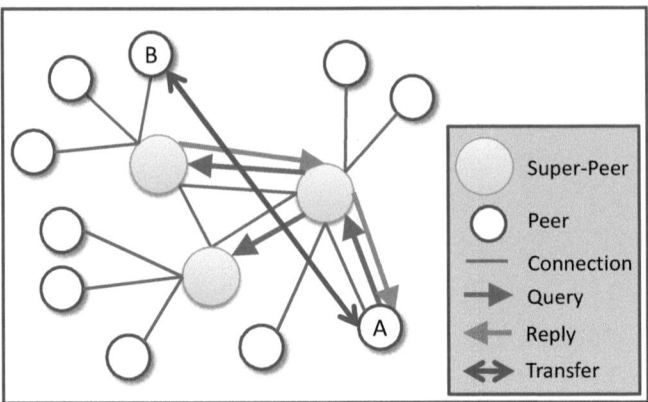

Figure 2.3: The super-peer concept

Napster, however it is far higher than in Gnutella while generating far less traffic on the network. This may be one of the reasons, why even today 2nd generation networks like eDonkey are still very common.

3rd Generation

Further improving the second generation approaches lead system engineers to the following design goals: complete decentralization, absolute equality, an efficient search and a reasonable scalability. To satisfy the first goal, the index of shared files need to be completely distributed. Until now, the index was either hosted completely on one server farm (see Napster) or there existed several independent indexes in the super-peer approach. Ion Stoica was the first to use the concept of distributed hash tables (DHT) and overcome this challenge with his P2P system Chord [20]. Chord uses a SHA-1-based [34] hash function $f_m(x)$ to map a key x onto the address space m. Additionally, this function is used to hash over the client's IP address and assign the resulting value to the peer's node ID in the interval between zero and $2^x - 1$. Each peer stores the part of the index with the keys lying in between its own address and the address of the peer with the largest ID smaller than its own. For information retrieval a peer uses the same hash function with some keywords as a parameter to calculate the corresponding key (see Fig. 2.4). We will describe this procedure in more detail in Section 2.2.

2.1 Peer-to-Peer Systems

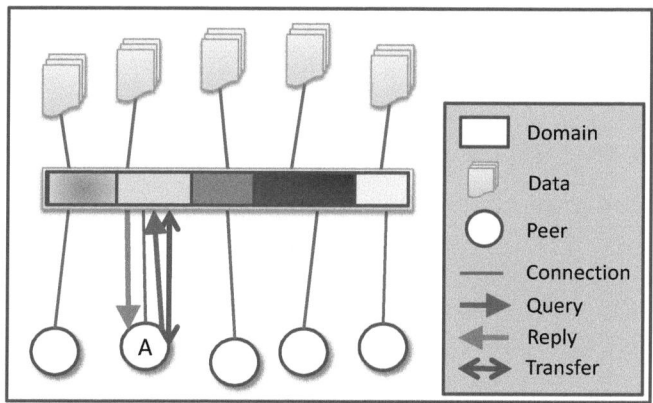

Figure 2.4: Use of distributed hash tables in P2P networks

By distributing the index over all peers, we successfully fulfilled the first design goal. Furthermore, we thereby conquer the remaining challenges as well. All peers are treated equal and run the same algorithm, hence we get absolute equality. In the following, we assume a network consisting of n nodes. By using a DHT, we divide the address space in sub spaces, enabling peers to efficiently search for a data element in $O(\log n)$. Whereas in earlier systems additional peers decreased the overall bandwidth per peer due to the limited capacity at the server (e.g. Napster's server or Kazaa's super-peer), in third generation P2P systems peers actually add to the overall resources. With each new peer comes new disk space and new computing power. Therefore, these systems overcome the scalability problems of older systems.

4th Generation

As the third generation of P2P systems has not yet conquered our everyday life, it is difficult to speculate about the future of P2P. Current research projects invest in many different areas, but it still remains open what the 4th generation of P2P will look like.

For some projects e.g. Freenet [29, 35], the next generation systems include mechanisms to secure the user's privacy. It is unique in the way it handles the storage of content as users disconnect after uploading their content. Once a file is uploaded, the content is mirrored and moved around the Freenet network, making it difficult to trace, or to destroy. The content will remain in the network for as long as people are retrieving it, although Freenet makes no guarantee that content will be stored indefinitely.

Other projects like the P2P Next [36] project pursue the goal of a zero-server environment. Therefore, the projects aims to develop a *next generation* Internet TV distribution system based on P2P and social interaction. Currently, the infrastructure of the Internet is not suited for simultaneous transmissions of live events to millions of people (i.e. broadcasting). The major problem is that a dedicated stream of data must be sent to every single user. With millions of potential users, the simultaneous streams of data easily congest the Internet. The P2P-Next project tries to advance in these important areas, including evolutionary content distribution, easy access to vast amount of content with metadata federation, and social networking.

2.2 Pastry - A Basis for Geostry

In this section, we describe a representative for a third generation P2P model in more detail. As Geostry builds on Pastry's [37], we illustrate their basic functionality with this system.

In 2001 Antony Rowstron and Peter Druschel developed Pastry, which meanwhile has become a representative for a scalable, decentralized object location and routing peer-to-peer system. Pastry performs application-level routing and object location even in very large overlay networks, consisting of peers which are interconnected via the Internet. The Pastry nodes thereby form a self-organizing and fault-tolerant network with a deterministic object location. Therefore, Pastry is used in a variety of peer-to-peer applications, such as SplitStream [38] (data distribution), SCRIBE [39] (group communication) or PAST [40] (global data storage).

2.2.1 Peer Setup

To participate in a Pastry peer-to-peer overlay network, each node is assigned a 128-bit node identifier (node ID). This node ID indicates a node's position in Pastry's circular ID-space, ranging from 0 to $2^{128} - 1$. Usually, node IDs are generated by applying a cryptographic hash function on the node's public key or its IP address.

2.2 Pastry - A Basis for Geostry

We therefore can assume that the node IDs are uniformly distributed in the ID-space. Furthermore, applying this assignment procedure with a high probability leads to the fact, that adjacent node IDs are diverse in geography, ownership, etc.

During runtime, each node maintains a state table, consisting of a *leaf-* and *neighborhood set*, as well as a *routing table*. Fig. 2.5 shows the exemplary state tables for a node with node ID 10233102.

The leaf set L comprises a set of nodes, namely $\frac{|L|}{2}$ nodes with the numerically closest larger node IDs, and the $\frac{|L|}{2}$ nodes with the numerically closest smaller node IDs based on the current node's node ID. The leaf set improves the routing efficiency and adds to its robustness. Furthermore, it may be used for fault detection, as the members of the leaf set mutually check the integrity through keep-alive mechanisms. The neighborhood set M consists of the $|M|$ nodes, which are the closest to the present node. Closest in this case refers a scalar proximity metric. By measuring the amount of IP hops or the *ping* delay, a node can probe the distance to other nodes (Locality). Whereas the leaf set is mainly used in message routing, the major task for the neighborhood set is to maintain locality properties. Typical values for $|L|$ and $|M|$ are 2^b or $2*2^b$ (b is a configuration parameter with the typical value 4).

The routing table R contains $\lceil \log_{2^b} n \rceil$ rows with $2^b - 1$ entries each. The entries at a row n in the routing table refer to nodes whose node IDs match the present node's node ID in the first n digits, but differs at the $n + 1$th digit. Each entry contains the IP addresses of one node with the appropriate prefix, ordered by the proximity metric. If the present node is not aware of nodes with a suitable node ID, the appropriate entry in the routing table is left empty. The uniform distribution of node ID ensures an even population of the routing table. Through the parameter b it is possible to decide on the trade-off between the amount of entries in the routing table (approximately $\lceil \log_{2^b} n \rceil * (2^b - 1)$ entries) and the maximum number of hops between any two nodes. For example, with a value of $b = 4$ and $N = 10^6$ nodes, the routing table will contain around 75 nodes on average and an expected hop count of 5, whilst with $N = 10^9$ nodes around 105 entries will populate the routing table, increasing the expected hop count to 7.

Nodeld 10233102			
Leaf set	SMALLER	LARGER	
10233033	10233021	10233120	10233122
10233001	10233000	10233230	10233232
Routing table			
-0-2212102	1	-2-2301203	-3-1203203
0	1-1-301233	1-2-230203	1-3-021022
10-0-31203	10-1-32102	2	10-3-23302
102-0-0230	102-1-1302	102-2-2302	3
1023-0-322	1023-1-000	1023-2-121	3
10233-0-01	1	10233-2-32	
0		102331-2-0	
		2	
Neighborhood set			
13021022	10200230	11301233	31301233
02212102	22301203	31203203	33213321

Figure 2.5: State of a Pastry node with node ID 10233102, b=2, and l=8 (base 4). Associated IP addresses are not shown. [40]

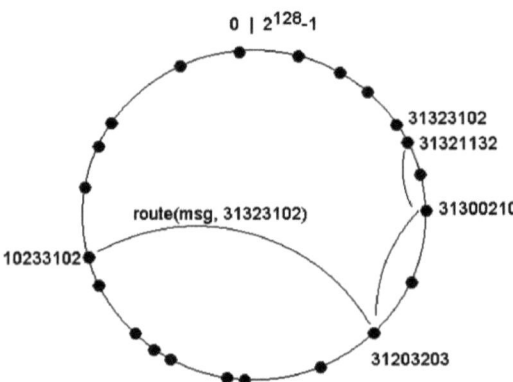

Figure 2.6: Routing a message from the node with node ID 10233102 with the key 31323102 [41]

Symbol	Description
R_l^i	entry in routing table R at column i, $0 \le i \le 2^b$ and row l, $0 \le l < \lfloor 128/b \rfloor$
L_i	i-th closest node ID in the leaf set L; positive/negative indices indicate node IDs with larger/smaller node IDs than present node ID
D_l	value of l-th digit in key D
$shl\,(A, B)$	length of prefix shared by A and B (in digits)

Table 2.1: Definitions for Pastry routing algorithm

2.2.2 Routing

Fig. 2.6 gives an example of the actions that occur when a node 10233102 routes a message to the node with the ID 31323102. In the following, we describe the routing protocol in more detail. Whenever a message with key D arrives at a node with node ID A the routing procedure (Algorithm 1) is executed.

Algorithm 1 Pseudo code for Pastry's routing algorithm

1: **procedure** Route(*message(key D)*)
2:   **if** $L_{-\lfloor |L|/2 \rfloor} \le D \le L_{+\lfloor |L|/2 \rfloor}$ **then**
3:      // use leaf set
4:      calculate L_i such that $|D - L_i|$ is minimal
5:      accept message if $L_i = currentPeer$, otherwise forward it to L_i
6:   **else**
7:      // use routing table
8:      Let $l = shl(D, A)$
9:      **if** $R_l^{D_l} \ne null$ **then**
10:        forward to $R_l^{D_l}$
11:      **else**
12:        // should only occur rarely
13:        forward to $T \in L \cup R \cup M$ such that
14:        $shl(T, D) \ge l$,
15:        $|T - D| < |A - D|$
16:      **end if**
17:   **end if**

At first, the node checks if the key falls into the range of the node IDs covered by its leaf set (line 2). If so, the message is forwarded to the one node in the leaf set with the node ID closest to to the key (line 4). In case the key is not covered by the leaf set, the routing table is used to distinguish the next node, the message is forwarded to. The present node searches its routing table for a node that shares a common prefix with the key by at least one more digit than itself (lines 7-9). In some cases it might occur that the routing table does either not include a suited entry or the associated node is not reachable. Then, the message is forwarded to a node that shares a prefix with the key at least as long as the present node, but whose node ID is numerically closer to the key than the present node's node ID (lines 12-14). Unless the message has already arrived at the node with the numerically closest node ID, such a node must exist in the leaf set. If not all adjacent nodes in the leaf set have failed simultaneously, at least one of the nodes is alive.

Routing Performance

It can be shown that in the average case, with accurate routing tables and no recent node failures, the expected number of routing steps is $\lceil \log_{2^b} n \rceil$. The routing algorithm offers three branches:

- The key lies within the leaf set. Therefore, the destination node is at most one hop away from the present node.

- The message is forwarded using the routing table. The amount of nodes whose node IDs have a longer prefix match with the key is reduced by the factor 2^b in each step. Thus, the destination is reached in $\lceil \log_{2^b} n \rceil$ steps.

- The leaf set does not cover the key and the routing table does not offer an entry for the appropriate prefix. Analysis has shown, that with a reasonable leaf set size ($|L| = 2^b$) this case is highly unlikely (less than two percent). Nevertheless, in most cases this case leads only to one additional routing step, as with a high probability the next node has some suitable nodes in its routing table.

In the unlikely event of many concurrent node failures, the number of routing steps may be at worst linear in n. However, as this is only the case while the nodes are updating their state and nodes with adjacent node IDs fail simultaneously, the probability of such a failure is kept very low.

2.2.3 Peer Operation

Apart from routing messages, Pastry nodes have to support further methods. Among these are procedures for joining and leaving an existing overlay network.

Joining

When a new node X wants to join a Pastry overlay network it has to inform other nodes of its presence and fill its state table. We assume that X is already aware of another node A, which participates in the network and resides in the proximity of X. Otherwise, X has to solve the bootstrapping problem (see Section 2.3) first. To commence the Join operation, X sends a special message - containing X as a key - to A requesting it to route this message. This message is then routing to node Z with the node ID numerically closest to X. In the highly unlikely event that $X = Z$, X must choose another node ID. As the message travels from A to Z, X copies the state tables from the intermediate nodes and thereby fills its own. Assuming X and A share no common prefix, we let A_i denote the i-th row of A's routing table. So, as the entries in row zero are independent of a node's node ID, A_0 contains appropriate values for X_0. However, as X and A share no common prefix, all other rows of A are of no use for X. Values for the next rows, e.g. X_1 can be taken from subsequent nodes, in this case from B_1. This is due to the fact, that the i-th row of the routing table from the i-th node (here: X_1 and B_1) share the same i-first digits in their node ID. Thereby, the X's routing table is filled. Finally, as the key X is numerically close to Z, X also obtains the leaf set from Z and similar to this, receives the neighborhood set from A, as A lies in the direct proximity of X. Using this information one can show that X can correctly initialize its state table and notify all necessary nodes of its arrival. Upon receiving the special update message, the other nodes in turn update their state tables as well. On average, the total cost for a node joining the overlay network is $O(\log_{2^b} n + |L| + |M|)$ in terms of exchanged messages.

Leaving

Nodes in the overlay network may fail or leave the network at any time. This entails several actions to correct the state tables at all participating nodes. In this scenario node A encounters a node failure.

To correct the leaf set, its neighbor in node ID space contacts the live node with the largest index on the side, where the node has failed. That is, if $L_i \lfloor |L|/2 < i < 0 \rfloor$ failed, the leaf set L' is requested from $L_{-|L|/2}$. L' most likely overlaps with the leaf set L from the present node, but it will also contain at least one new node. The most appropriate node is then contacted and if alive chosen to replace the failed node. Unless $\lfloor |L|/2 \rfloor$ nodes fail simultaneously, this healing mechanism eventually repairs each node's leaf set, even for small values for $|L|$.

Routing table failures are only observed in the routing process, more precisely node A tries to route a message to node B and receives no response from it. In this case, A simply chooses the next best node from its state table to forward the message to. However, the routing table entry needs to be corrected to preserve its integrity. The failed routing table entry R_l^d can be repaired as follows: the present node contacts a node $R_l^i, i \neq d$ of the same row and asks for that node's entry for R_l^d. In case no entry in row l has a pointer to a live node with the appropriate prefix, the node checks the next rows $R_{l+1}^i, i \neq d$ to enhance the scope. Thereby, an appropriate node - if existing - is very likely to be found.

Though the neighborhood set is not involved in the routing process, it is viable to keep an up-to-date view on nearby nodes. Thereby, a node contacts its neighbors periodically to check their liveness. If a node does not respond to the ping, A asks other nodes from its neighborhood table for their neighbors. Afterwards, it checks those neighbors for their distance and updates its neighborhood set accordingly.

2.3 Bootstrapping in Decentralized Systems

The term *bootstrapping* denotes a process starting a complex system with a simple one. In many cases, it is the solution for the hen and egg problem - where the consequence is the root cause - to start a system through itself. In computer science, the term describes the starting of a computer, where we need a mechanism (e.g. BIOS) to start further software (e.g. the operating system). The simple program that actually begins the initialization of the computer's operating system (like LILO, NTLDR or GRUB) is also called *bootstrap*.

In the field of distributed systems, the term still describes the way of starting a system. However, it is related to computer networks. When we want to set up a peer-to-peer network for a certain purpose, we have to be aware of two things:

1. *Existence*
   Does this network already exist? If not, then we create a new P2P network. Leaving other possible participants with the next question.

2. *Address*

Where do we find other members of the P2P system? In a DHT-based P2P system there is no centralized component storing an index of active peers.

The key question therefore is: how does a suitable mechanism to bootstrap peers in a P2P network look like. A lot of research has been done on this field (see Section 6.2), however most projects rely on a centralized component. Gnutella for example uses a hard-coded IP address to contact a server providing a list of recently active peers [3]. Other authors propose bootstrapping methods basing on Multicast [42] or Anycast [43]. Those approaches face certain problems in the current IP v4 architecture and therefore do not solve the bootstrapping problem entirely. We present a novel solution to this problem in Chapter 3.

2.4 Location-based Services

In 2000 large telecom providers like Ovum initially defined location-based services by "network-based services that integrate a derived estimate of a mobile device's location or position with other information so as to provide value to the user" [44]. Soon after this Ericsson Consulting however declared that LBS are not short range radio (e.g. Bluetooth) or cell broadcast services. Other industry players came up with their own ideas, basing an LBS on a mix of equipment, activities and goods.

In science we can find numerous definitions for context-based systems (CBS), e.g. in [45–47]. [48] defines context as the information used to characterize the situation of an entity. These entities are persons, locations, or objects considered to be relevant for the behavior of an application. More general, CBS pose an extension to location-based services as they do take various other aspects into account, for instance time (present, future and/or past) or a combination of already given context-information (e.g. location and time; identity, location and time). However, a thorough examination of the possibilities of CBS is out of scope of this. We concentrate on a subset of context-based systems, namely the location-based services.

For the remainder of the book, we assume that LBS always include the following three activities:

1. Calculate the location of the consumer
2. Produce a service based on this location

3. Deliver this location enhanced service to others

Fig 2.7 shows the functionality of the location service. The available means for positioning (wireless, GPS, etc.) are combined with information about certain events (temperature, images, restaurant recommendations, etc.) offering this data via a location service.

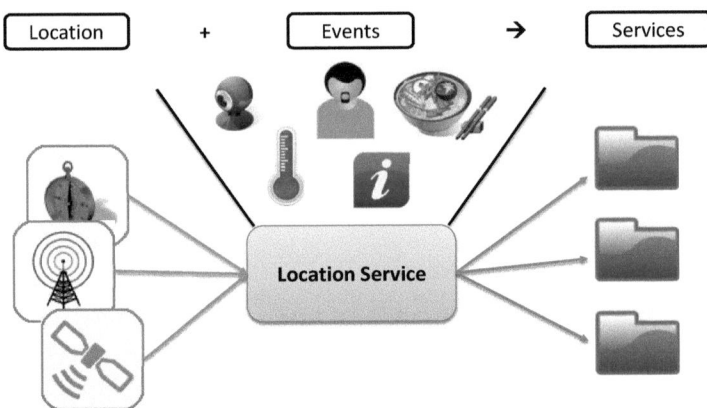

Figure 2.7: The location service architecture

2.4.1 Location Modeling

Location modeling poses an essential topic in the field of pervasive computing. Today, system developers may rely on different sensing technologies to acquire spatial information. Location plays an important role in context-based systems and is used in a variety of applications for purposes such as position determination, navigation, routing, tracking, monitoring of pervasive computing devices and many others.

To guarantee the success of such a pervasive application, it is essential to set a high value on the system design. Therefore, the underlying coordinate system has to be chosen carefully to ensure that the application on top is able to provide all necessary information.

Coordinates of a distinct coordinate system are used to define the position of a point in space. For complicated spaces (e.g. the surface of Earth) it is sometimes very difficult if not impossible to provide a single consistent coordinate space. To overcome this problem, several coordinate systems - each for a distinct region - are used together to form an atlas covering the entire space.

Some of the properties of coordinate systems influence the way they can be used:

- *Human readability:* Some coordinates can be given in a human understandable way (e.g. symbolic coordinates). This might make it easier for humans to work with an application, basing on such coordinates. Applications using GPS-coordinates are far more difficult for humans to handle.

- *Exactness:* The exactness of the given information may become important in navigation. However, calculating the distance between two symbolic coordinates requires a sophisticated underlying model. Only then, it is possible to answer *nearest neighbor* queries.

- *Singularities:* Coordinate systems suffer from *singularities*. Then, a position in space has multiple coordinates. For example, the origin in the *polar coordinate system* (r, θ) by definition has the value $(r = 0)$ for the radial coordinate. However, the angle can have any value and still refer to the origin.

In mathematics and its application we can find a multitude of coordinate systems. One of the most common ones is the Cartesian coordinate system as in Fig. 2.8. It is mostly used for a two- or three dimensional flat space and uses two respectively three numbers to represent the distance to the origin. For the use in our scenario, the Cartesian coordinate system is not the optimal choice. Therefore, we take a look at other more promising coordinate systems presented in [49, 50].

Symbolic Coordinates

In symbolic coordinate systems, locations are described by an abstract identifier, the so-called *symbolic coordinate*. Though, symbolic coordinates pose some problems as they offer no spatial relation. For example, it is difficult to calculate the remaining distance between the 'playground' and the 'shopping center'. On the other hand, they incorporate some obvious advantages. For instance, the symbolic coordinates are human readable, which can be helpful in terms of navigation. It is much easier for a child to go to the "playground" instead of going to *48°47'44" N, 9°28'55" E*. Symbolic coordinate systems can be found in the following models (also see Fig 2.9):

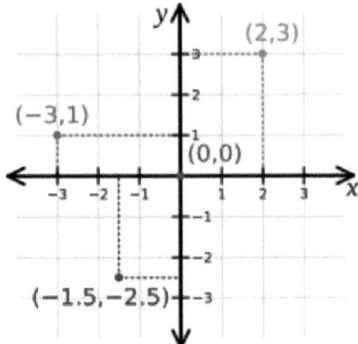

Figure 2.8: Cartesian coordinate system in a plane [51]

- *Simple symbolic model or cell model:* In this model, a coordinate stands for an arbitrary geographic region. Inclusions are not accounted for in this model.

- *Exclusive symbolic model or zone model:* This model adds a restriction to the former model. The regions now have to be disjunct.

- *Location tree:* This model enhances the zone model by enabling the user to model a complete overlap of two areas. In doing so, we get a tree-like structure and a hierarchy of symbolic coordinates.

- *Acyclic location graph or domain model:* Here, symbolic coordinates may describe an arbitrary region. Thus, in this model all types of inclusion (none, partial, complete) can be modeled between any region. Therefore, this model poses an enhancement to the cell model.

Geometric Coordinates

Geometric coordinates are used to describe a location through an n-tuple. With sets of coordinate n-tuples points, areas or volumes can be represented. We thereby distinguish between two model types:

- *Simple geometric model:* The simple model bases on a single reference coordinate system (RCS), e.g. using latitude and longitude (see Section 2.6.1).

2.4 Location-based Services

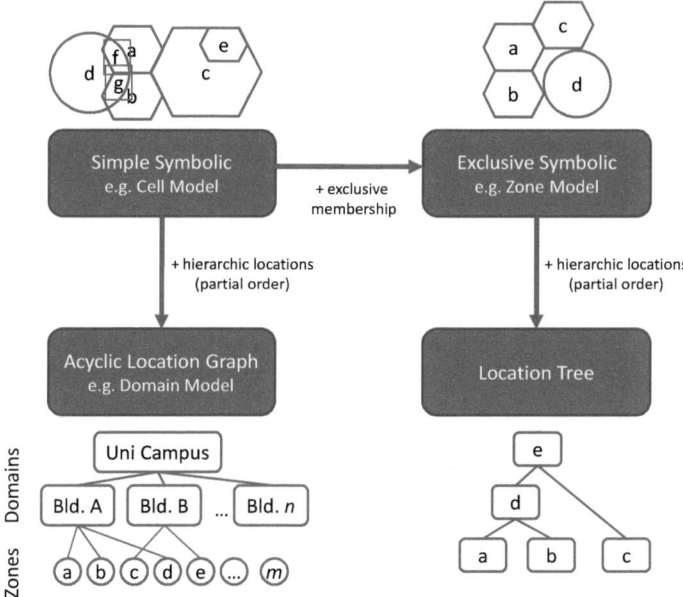

Figure 2.9: Symbolic Models [50]

- *Unified geometric model:* This model type combines multiple reference coordinate systems. Usually, this is done to increase the accuracy of the position. Imagine tracking a user through wireless triangulation [52]. It is difficult to determine the level the user is in, so combining this systems with other systems, e.g. a smart floor [53], improves the accuracy.

Geometric functions, such as the Euclidian distance enable the calculation of distances between arbitrary points, thus allowing for *nearest neighbor* queries. To allow for *range queries*, it is essential to determine whether ranges are included in each other. This can be realized by specifying the geometric extension of a geometric figure, e.g. through the overlap of geometric figures. In Section 2.6.1, we give a more detailed view on the use of geometric coordinates in reference to locations on Earth.

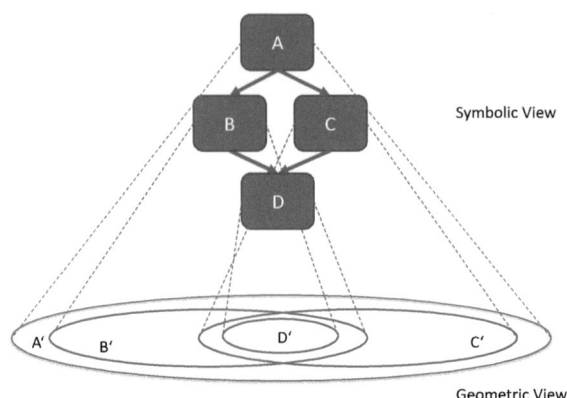

Figure 2.10: Hybrid Model [50]

Hybrid Models

Hybrid models - also called *semi-symbolic model* combine both models mentioned above (see Fig. 2.10). Located objects are represented by both included models: the object has a symbolic name with a membership in one or more location domains and area coordinates of an RCS from the geometric model.

Location Association

According to [49] a location can be associated with an object in two different ways:

- *Positioning:* The position of an object is given in relation to a frame of reference (usually through a grid). The resolution is defined by the grid spacing and allows the current position of an object to be represented by a set of coordinates. Relations between different objects respectively between their locations can be expressed by the Euclidian distance between them.

- *Containment:* Expressing object locations through containment relations may not be as intuitive as through explicit positioning, however it is essential for answering spatial queries (see Section 2.4.2). The position of an object is identified by the spatial region which contains the object. That is, a location encloses other objects, e.g. a floor contains several rooms. Enclosed objects can but do not need to be organized hierarchically. In this case, the exactness of the location depends on the size of the container enclosing the object.

2.4.2 Spatial Queries

A *spatial query* typically represents a special database query supported by spatial (or geo-) databases. Those queries differ from standard SQL queries by the supported data types. Spatial databases allow geometry data types such as points, lines and polygons and consider the spatial relationship between these geometries. As we have seen in the previous section, those queries may include functions like `distance`, `intersects`, `contains`, etc. For the remainder of the book, we focus on the following more user-intuitive spatial queries using the example in Figure 2.11.

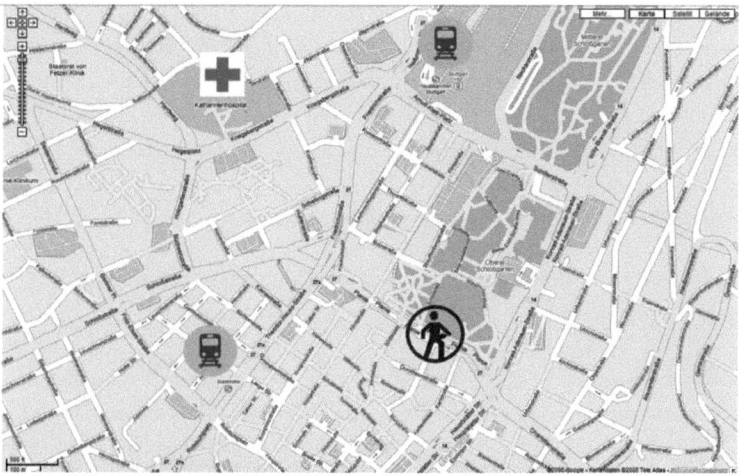

Figure 2.11: Map of Stuttgart, Germany

- *Position Queries* retrieve the position of an object, e.g. "where is Martin", or "what is the position of the Katharinenhospital".

- *Nearest Neighbor Queries* provide a set of one or more objects that are closest to the position of another object. Thus, they allow for queries for the nearest train station, restaurant, hotel, etc.

- *Range Queries* offer a set of objects, which are currently located in a spatial range. For example, "what objects can be found on the 3rd floor of the BC building" returns all objects on the floor as well as in the rooms.

2.5 Linearization

In computer science, we often have to deal with multi-dimensional data. Popular representatives are *vectors, matrices, image data, tables of relational databases, or coordinates*. Working with this kind of data poses some difficulty when applying certain operations, e.g. the sequential traversal of data or the process, when data from main memory is written to disk. The necessary step to overcome this difficulty is often referred to as *linearization*.

In this book, we are dealing with location-based information. This information may originate from anywhere in the world. As we do not want to use Earth's actual shape as a reference coordinate system (the shape is too complex, it's not even a sphere), we use a projection (see Section 2.6 for details) to map Earth's surface to a 2D field. As peer-to-peer systems use a one-dimensional structure (in Pastry we use a ring structure) we need to map Earth's 2D coordinates to Pastry's 1D ring structure. Therefore, we search for a suitable linearization technique.

In the following, we describe the functional requirements that need to be fulfilled for a successful linearization [54]:

- *Unique Indexing:* It is essential, that the linearization process assigns each data element a unique index. This ensures, that the data written from memory to hard disk can be loaded back to memory without integrity errors. Furthermore, the index ensures that each data element is read only once during the traversal.

- *Continuity:* To efficiently linearize a coherent dataset, the resulting index needs to be coherent to. The resulting index thus ranges from 0 to $n-1$ without any "holes" in it.

The following requirements are not vital, however they may improve the efficiency when applying the linearization process to a specific field of application:

2.5 Linearization

- *Costs:* The mapping during the process needs to be computable at low cost. If the mapping gets too expensive it may outweigh the advantages of linearization.

- *Locality:* Data fragments being close in multi-dimensional space shall be still close after linearization. This feature becomes important whenever adjacent data is read simultaneously (e.g. extraction of an image section) or in sequence. Then, the locality of data then greatly improves the cache performance.

- *Equality:* The linearization process should not privilege or penalize a single dimension. Usually, this feature does not play a big role, however in case the predictability of a program gets interesting, equality gains in importance.

One of the most straight-forward solutions would be to enumerate data along its lines and columns. Using the image processing example, this would mean to read all pixels from left to right and line-by-line from top to bottom. Though this method is easy to compute it fulfills the locality property only partially. Data in the same line is still adjacent, whereas data from adjacent lines is at least m (the number of elements in a line) elements away. Using the line-by-line linearization also leads to the fact that the equality requirement does not stand.

Therefore, we need another linearization technique, which can be found in the subject of space-filling curves (SFC). SFCs have generated a great deal of interest since Peano discovered the first curve around 100 years ago. Soon after, other prominent mathematicians such as Hilbert, Sierpinski, and Lebesgue also made significant contributions to the field.

2.5.1 Space-filling Curves

It was Georg Cantor's finding in 1878 which started it all. By then, he demonstrated that any two finite-dimensional smooth manifolds - regardless their dimensions - have the same cardinality. This implies, that the interval $[0, 1]$ can be mapped bijectively in any finite-dimensional manifold, such as a square $[0, 1]^2$. Thereby, he showed that the uniform interval contains as many points as the uniform square, though the interval is a proper subset of the square. Immediately after this finding, the question whether such a mapping could be continuous arose. In 1879 Eugen Netto gave the mathematical proof, that such a bijective mapping is necessarily discontinuous. The condition for bijectivity was then dropped and the search for a curve passing through every point (surjectivity) of an n-dimensional region continued. In 1890, it was Giuseppe Peano who discovered such a continuous surjective mapping, thereby finding the "first" space-filling curve. As Peano was the first to find such a curve in 2-dimensional space, space-filling curves are sometimes also called *Peano Curves*.

Until then, mathematician considered curves to be "1-dimensional" and "thin", not being able to fill a unit square. Therefore, Peano's curves added new aspects and soon after other mathematicians deducted other continuous curves. Peano's example was also extended to fill any n-dimensional $(n > 0)$ space entirely.

To correctly define a space-filling curve, we first have to give a mathematical definition of a curve. Mathematically, a curve results from a mapping of a parameter interval in an area or a volume.

Definition 2.1 (Curve)
Let $f : \Im \to \mathbb{R}^n$ be a continuous mapping of the set $\Im \subset \mathbb{R}$ into $\mathbb{R}^n$. Then the appropriate image $f_*(\Im)$ of the mapping denotes a curve, and the representation $x = f(t), t \in \Im$ is called parametric representation of the curve.

The *image* of a mapping is defined as the set of possible values denoted by $f_*(\Im) := \{f(x) \in \mathbb{R}^n | x \in \Im\}$. For the set of parameters $\Im$ we consider intervals, such as the uniform interval $[0,1]$ or more complex sets. For the remainder of the book, we consider each curve filling an area or a volume completely a *space-filling curve*.

Definition 2.2 (Space-filling Curve)
The curve $f_*(\Im)$ of a mapping $f : \Im \to \mathbb{R}^n$ is called a space-filling curve if $f_*(\Im)$ has a Jordan content (area for $n = 2$, volume for $n = 3$, ...) greater than 0.

The mapping $f : \Im \to \Gamma \subset \mathbb{R}^n$ is *surjective* if any value of the subset Γ is taken. If Γ's area (or the volume) is larger than 0, then $f_*(\Im)$ is a space-filling curve. Further information can be found in [55] or [56].

2.5.2 Lindenmayer Systems

A *Lindenmayer system* (short: *L-System*) is a parallel rewriting system. It consists of a set of rules and symbols, thus representing a formal grammar. They were developed in 1968 by Aristid Lindenmayer, a biologist and botanist from the University of

2.5 Linearization

Utrecht, Netherlands. The L-systems became popular as they allowed for a simple modeling of the growth process of plants and modeling of the morphology of various organisms [57]. Later the system was extended and could also be used to generate self-similar Fractals, such as space-filling curves.

Definition 2.3 (Definition of an L-System)
An L-System is a quadruple $G = (V, S, \omega, P)$ with

- ***V*** *is the alphabet (set of symbols) containing elements that can be replaced (like variables)*

- ***S*** *is a set of symbols containing elements that remain fixed (like constants)*

- *ω represents the start/axiom and consists of a string of variables from **V**, thereby defining the initial state of the system*

- ***P*** *is a set of production rules defining how variables can be replaced with constants and variables. A production consists of a predecessor and a successor*

The example below shows the creation of Fibonacci numbers, where G is defined by $V = \{A, B\}, S = \{\}, \omega = A, P = \{(A \rightarrow B), (B \rightarrow AB)\}$. In the following, the o denotes the *order* or iteration of the production rules. Counting the length of the strings, we get the Fibonacci sequence (see brackets).

- $o = 0$: A (1)
- $o = 1$: B (1)
- $o = 2$: AB (2)
- $o = 3$: BAB (3)
- $o = 4$: ABBAB (5)
- $o = 5$: BABABBAB (8)

To illustrate the representation of an L-System we use Turtle. Turtle Graphic - a component of the programming language Logo [58] developed by Daniel G. Bobrow - allows for a simple generation of plants, various other geographic forms, and space-filling curves.

Table 2.2 shows a few examples and gives the corresponding production rules. In these examples the constants $S = +, -$ are used to "turn the turtle" left respectively to the right using the specified angle.

2.6 Map Projections

In this section we give a short introduction into the science of map making, also called *cartography*. This research area deals with a variety of problems, such as measuring Earth's shape and its features, adapting three-dimensional features to flat models or devising conventions for a graphical representation of data. In the following we inform about the different cartographic concepts, explain how maps are drawn and give examples for the various projections for world maps. However, we will not go into much detail, further information can be found in [60, 61].

2.6.1 Basic Definitions

Shape of the Earth

Our planet Earth is the largest stone-based planet in our solar system. All larger planets mainly consist out of gas, which is compressed heavily in the planet's interior. This may be one of the reasons why Earth is not perfectly round. Furthermore, the rotation effects are flattening the poles and bulging the equator, forming Earth's shape very close to an *oblate spheroid*. However, Earth's mass concentration is not uniform, due to an irregular land distribution and crust density, resulting in an actual shape (of the *Geoid*), which varies by up to 100 meters [62].

In planetary dimensions, some local deviations can be ignored, such as the tallest land peak (Mount Everest: 8,848 m above local sea level) and the deepest undersea spot (Mariana Trench: 10,911 m below local sea level). Compared to a perfect ellipsoid, Earth's tolerance is far below 0.2 %, making the deviations insignificant.

For the maps covering larger areas, we assume Earth's shape to be perfectly spherical, since most of the shape imprecisions are negligible compared to the errors in the data and media resolutions. For maps covering small areas measurements may be based on a flat Earth, as terrain features dominate.

2.6 Map Projections

Nr.	Projection	Name	Description
A		Bush 1	$Start =$ " $+++++SLFFF$", $Order = 11$, $Angle = 18°$, $Rules = (S \to$ "$[++ +G][---G]TS$", $G \to$ " $+H[-G]L$", $H \to$ " $-G[+H]L$", $T \to$ "TL", $L \to$ "$[-FFF][+FFF]F$")
B		Bush 2	$Start =$ " $+++++++G$", $Order = 8$, $Angle = 180/14°$, $Rules = (G \to$ "$GFX[++G][--G]$", $X \to$ "$X[--FFF][++FFF]FX$")
C		Sierpinski Triangle	$Start =$ "$FXF--FF--FF$", $Order = 6$, $Angle = 60°$, $Rules = (F \to$ "FF", $X \to$ " $--FXF++FXF++FXF--$")
D		Spiral	$Start =$ "A", $Order = 18$, $Angle = 20°$, $Rules = (A \to$ "$[-A]F+F+F+F+F+F+F+F+F+F+F+F+F+F+F+F+F+F$")
E		Hilbert	$Start =$ "L", $Order = 6$, $Angle = 90°$, $Rules = (L \to$ " $+RF-LFL-FR+$", $R \to$ " $-LF+RFR+FL-$")
F		H-curve	$Start =$ " $+H$", $Order = 4$, $Angle = 90°$, $Rules = (F \to$ "FF", $H \to$ " $+F+FH++FFH++F+FF+FH++FFH++F+F-$")

Table 2.2: Samples of Lindenmayer Systems [59]

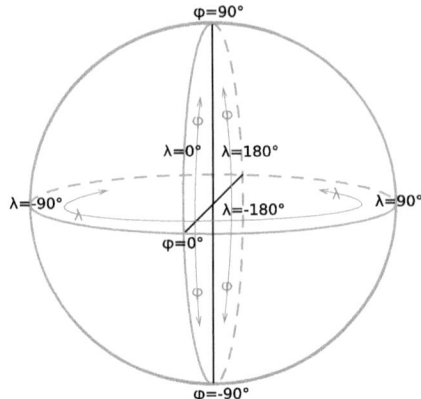

Figure 2.12: Latitude phi (ϕ) and longitude lambda (λ) [63]

Coordinate System

To exactly specify a location on Earth, we have to use a geographic coordinate system. Therefore, three types of coordinates are used: longitude, latitude and geodesic height. The coordinate systems classifies Earth in 360 degrees of longitude (abbreviation: Long. or λ) and 180 degrees of latitude (abbreviation: Lat. or ϕ). The equator is the fundamental plane the geographic coordinate system as it divides the globe into the Northern and Southern Hemispheres. Thus, latitude starts at the equator with 0° and reaches 90°N at the north pole and 90°S at the south pole. Longitude uses a randomly chosen starting point as zero-longitude reference line. Currently, international standards use the Royal Observatory in Greenwich, UK as the Prime Meridian. Longitude starts there with 0° and lasts 180°E (eastwards) and 180°W (westwards). An illustration of the coordinate system can be seen in Fig.2.12.

To specify a location most accurately, we have to add topological information. This defines the vertical distance from the center of the sphere (*vertical datum*) or the surface of the sphere (*mean sea level*). Aside from very deep positions and positions in space, the vertical datum is rather uncommon. The mean sea level however is not defined equally all over the world. Each country has defined its own reference point, e.g. the United Kingdom's is Newlyn.

Projections

The world we live in roughly is a round globe. Working with a globe however is impractical, whereas flat maps often suffer from severe errors. Thus, map creation has to deal with certain trade-offs to optimally achieve the design goals. The process which converts features from a spherical or ellipsoidal surface onto a projection surface is called cartographical map projection. Many of those projections have been developed over the years, however only a few of them are widespread.

We usually generate a projection surface by 'touching´ the mapped sphere in one (surface is tangent) or more (surface is secant) regions. Regions close to the touching area are less distorted from the original spherical hull than those farther away. Some projections apply several surfaces to different regions of the map to reduce the error at the cost of complexity. Regardless the effort, projections can never perfectly convert a surface's feature to a flat map. At least one region of a planar map suffers from *distortion* when projecting a sphere. Distortions are present in false angles, shapes, areas, distances and in any degree of combination. Each map has its own characteristic distortion pattern, as can be seen in Section 2.6.3.

Another important factor is the orientation of the projections surface in respect to the original sphere. A distinct projection may be applied in several different *aspects*, defined by the graticule layout and the center of the map. Some of the more common aspects include the *polar* map (Earth's axis is aligned with the projection system, putting one of the poles in the center), the *equatorial* map (the equator is aligned with the map's horizontal axis), and the *oblique* map (axes are neither aligned with the polar nor with the equator). The polar aspect is mostly used for the azimuthal and conic groups of projections, while the equatorial is common for cylindrical and pseudocylindrical groups.

2.6.2 Map Properties

Each projection comes with different properties, and thus is only suitable for distinct purposes. Only a globe preserves all of Earth's features, since for that case no projection is involved, only a reduction is used. However a globe is too bulky, expensive to produce, unfeasible for reproduction in printed or electronic media etc., therefore making maps indispensable. Map properties can be expressed using the following parameters:

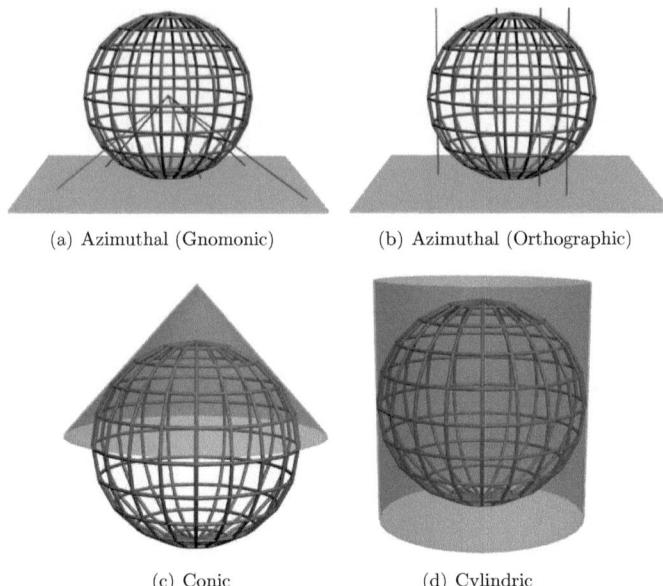

(a) Azimuthal (Gnomonic)   (b) Azimuthal (Orthographic)

(c) Conic   (d) Cylindric

Figure 2.13: Illustration of common projections using planes, cones and cylinders [64]

Preserving Distances

Any world map scales earth with a great reduction to have a map with a manageable size. Only a 'true' globe allows a constant scaling factor for any two points on Earth. In flat maps the scale will differ, depending on the direction and location. As a result scaling rulers can only be used to rather estimate than precisely calculate the distance between two points on the map (see Fig. 2.14).

Preserving Directions

Maps preserving directions are especially important when traveling over great distances (e.g. by plane, by ship). The problem is that in most map projections, directions are seldom preserved, making it difficult to determine the course (bearing) between two points. A *loxodrome* represents the easiest route for that, since is bears a constant course. Any loxodrome winds from pole to pole in a so called *spherical helix* as can be seen in the orthographical projection in Fig. 2.15(a) Mercator's conformal cylindrical projection has been revolutionary as any straight line

2.6 Map Projections

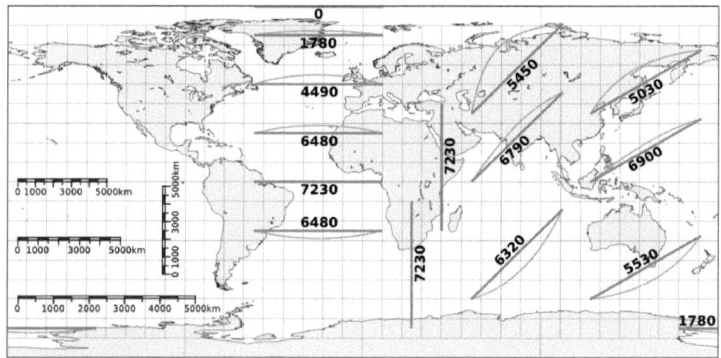

Figure 2.14: Distances in a cylindrical map [60] (curves representing geodesics)

between two points is a loxodrome. However, this projection is not sufficient for navigation as the polar regions are heavily distorted (see Fig. 2.15(b)). The blue lines shows a loxodrome, starting in Campinas, Brazil with a constant course of 60° clockwise from the true North.

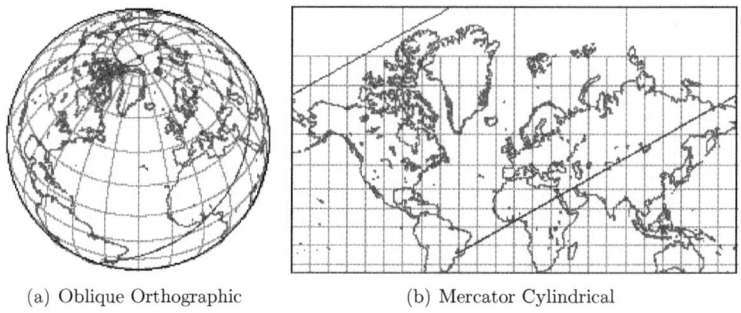

(a) Oblique Orthographic (b) Mercator Cylindrical

Figure 2.15: Illustration of loxodromes [60]

Preserving Areas

In most cases this is the most significant map property as those maps properly display true area ratios. Therefore, scientific applications (e.g. geographical distributions of population, pollution etc.) and educational atlases make heavy use of those maps. Much to the regret of cartographs, schools often use Mercator's projection in wall maps. Mercator's map is conformal, however increasingly stretches the surface towards the poles (see Fig. 2.16(a)). Fig. 2.16(b) shows that the Mollweide elliptical projection shows the size proportions correctly in this area. However, Mollweide suffers from a vertical distortion along the Equator.

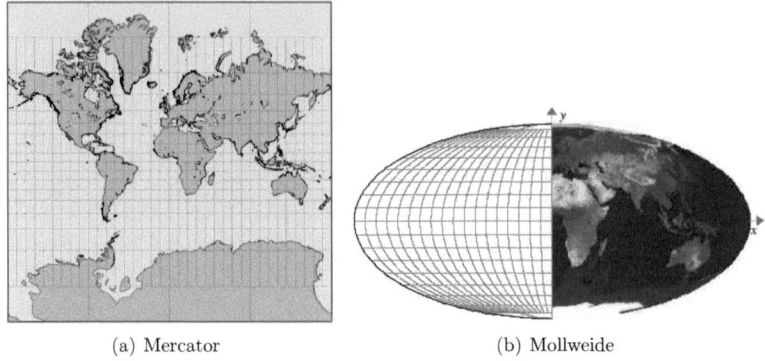

(a) Mercator   (b) Mollweide

Figure 2.16: Distortions of equal-area projections [60]

Equivalent (also called equal-area, equiareal or authalic) projections preserve areal relationships. That is, two regions r_1 and r_2 on Earth and their corresponding regions r'_1 and r'_2 on an equivalent map share an identical surface ratio, namely $\frac{r_1}{r'_1}$ and $\frac{r_2}{r'_2}$.

Geodesics

To solve the problem of finding the shortest paths between two points (e.g. in aviation), maps with *Great Circle Paths* have been invented. However, again there is no map showing true geodesics between any two points. Fig. 2.17 shows an example of an equatorial Mollweide projection (graticule spacing 15°), preserving area ratios, but no directions. The farther away from the center of the map, the greater the distortion. Therefore, we translate the map - such that the region of interest is centered - before we apply the projection. The red line shows the shortest path / great circle line between Campinas, Brazil and Tokyo, Japan. Azimuth projections can show great circle paths through a straight line, however they are not commonly used as they show true directions from the center point only.

2.6 Map Projections

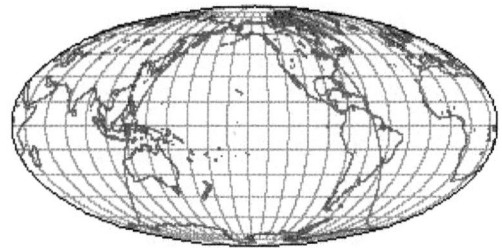

Figure 2.17: Equatorial Mollweide Projection with Geodesics [60]

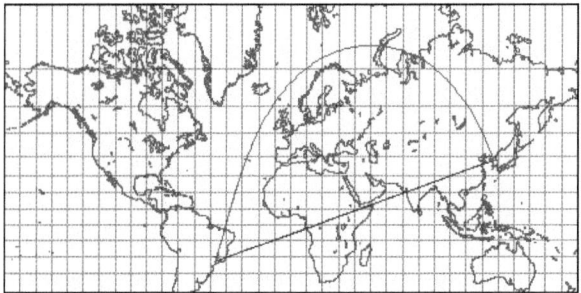

Figure 2.18: Mercator map showing a geodesic (arc) and loxodrome (line) [60]

Preserving Shapes

Conformal maps (e.g. azimuthal stereographic or Mercator) are locally preserving angles. As a result, any two lines in the map follow the same angle as the according lines on Earth. Furthermore, the scale at any particular point is the same in all directions, though it differs for different regions on the map.

As the shapes are preserved, conformal maps are often used for navigation. We illustrate the usage of loxodromes (blue line) and geodesics (red curve) in Fig. 2.18. The loxodrome plots a course from Campinas, Brazil to Seoul, South Korea with a constant bearing from any meridian. Thus, an aircraft would land safely using this fixed course (disregarding traffic airlines, weather, wind etc.). However, this is not the most economical choice as the shortest route follows the geodesic. Therefore, the pilot has to deal with a trade-off. Flying along the geodesic and doing constant course corrections or following the loxodrome while wasting fuel and time.

General Distortion Pattern

As every flat map comes with a distortion of some kind (shape, area or length), Nicolas Tissot developed a tool which today is known as *Tissot's indicatrix*. After drawing a circle upon an original sphere and mapping it to a flat surface, the circle may (depending on the chosen projection):

- change its size, thus suffering from a scale distortion
- loose its original shape
- stay free of distortions

Since some regions may be free of distortions, while others suffer from severe error, we draw very small circles all over the sphere to get a map expressing the distortion pattern. Fig. 2.19(a) shows the non-conformal Hammer map. Aside from the immediate center, all circles are deformed, however cover the exact same area, as this is an equivalent projection. The popular Mercator projection 2.19(b) is conformal, thus all circles keep their shape and meridians are always perpendicular to every parallel. However, areas are not preserved, which can be seen in the growing circle size towards the poles.

2.6.3 Projection Groups

Approaches to decide on one globally valid classification for map projection have not been successful yet. Therefore, we can find several (mostly orthogonal) arrangements with the effect that a single projection simultaneously may be part of several categories. In the last section we have classified projections by their properties. In this section we will give a classification by geometry followed by a summary of common map projections [1].

Classification by Geometry

Azimuthal projections preserve the azimuth in regard to a reference point (usually the center of the map). Therefore, it shows true directions to any other point,

---
[1] All images have been created with Vimage [65]

2.6 Map Projections

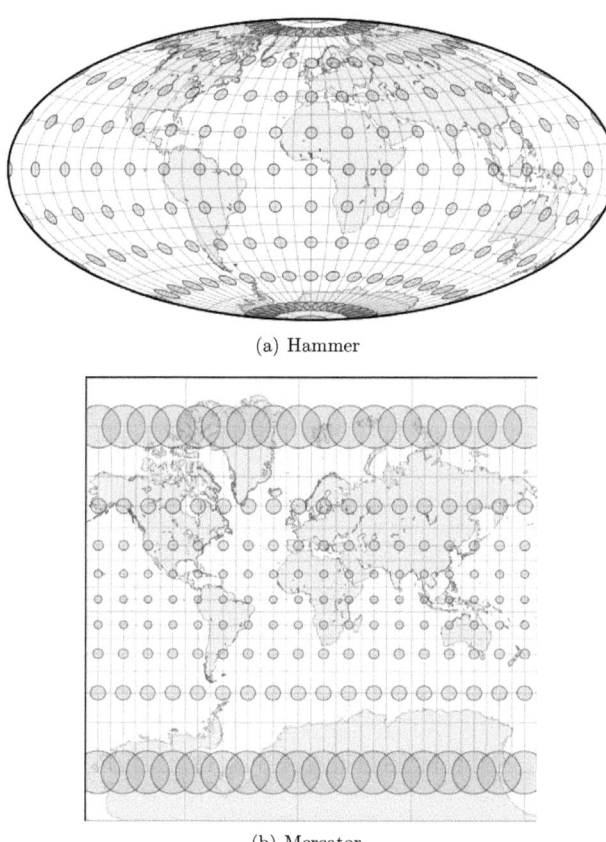

(a) Hammer

(b) Mercator

Figure 2.19: Tissot Indicatrices in the Hammer and the Mercator (clipped at 85°N/85°S) map [60]

however the distance may be altered. By choosing different perspectives, three azimuthal designs can be easily generated: gnomonic, orthographic, and stereographic (see C-E in Tab. 2.3). Regarding the polar aspect, one of the poles becomes the central point, effecting the graticule as follows: Meridians are straight lines, originating from the central point, while parallels become complete central circles. The center of the map plays an important role, as all straight lines passing through it are geodesics. Furthermore, the distortion in this projection also depends on the distance from the center.

Cylindrical projections use a cylinder as projection surface. In the most common equatorial aspect of this projection group all coordinate lines are straight and parallels intersect meridians always at right angles. Additionally, all parallels and meridians have the same length, giving world maps a rectangular shape. The scale on the parallels differs hugely (in fact reaches infinity at the pole), as on Earth the parallels have zero length at the poles but are as long as the Equator on the cylindrical map. Most projections in this group only differ slightly in the spacing of parallels. Some of the projections have become quite popular, as the Mercator or plate carrée (see G in Tab. 2.4) maps.

Pseudocylindrical or polycylindrical projections attempt to overcome the strong shape distortion of the cylindrical projections (see J in Tab. 2.4). In the normal equatorial aspect, projections share straight (however not necessarily equidistant) horizontal parallels, whereas the meridians are arbitrarily curved. As meridians and parallels do not always cross at right angles, pseudocylindrical maps are not conformal and usually suffer from a strong shape distortion at the polar regions. Many polycylindrical projections were designed for equivalence and therefore are a popular choice for world maps. Some of the more common maps include Mollweide and Eckert family.

Conic projections use a conic projection surface, giving maps the shape of a sector of circle (see F in Tab. 2.3). Regarding the regular polar aspect, meridians are straight equidistant lines which converge at a single point. This may or may not be the pole, depending on the projection parameters. The meridians converge due to the special cone constant which reduces the angular distance between them by a fixed factor. Parallels become arcs of circles, crossing all meridians at right angles. As a result, the scale is constant along each parallel. Due to their inherent distortion pattern conic maps have often been used to display national maps rather than world maps.

2.7 Replication

Pseudoconic projections differ from conic projections in the fact, that meridians may deviate from straight lines. In polar and equatorial aspects parallels are circular arcs and share a common central point. Pseudoconic maps (e.g. Tab. 2.4's I and K projection) differ greatly in shape, some have a rectangular or elliptical shape, while others are not even convex.

Other or arbitrary projections includes arbitrarily curved parallels and meridians. In most cases, there is no defined geometric construction as these projections are purely made to fit a custom purpose.

2.6.4 Summary

Unfortunately, there is no projection fulfilling all of the properties listed in the preceding sections. Most of the features are mutually exclusive, which is why we need to focus on our special scenario to then find the best map.

The major requirements for a fair distribution of load among all peers is the preservation of distances (scale), areas (distortion) and shapes (conformality). Fulfilling these requirements on the entire map makes sure, that peers on diverse spots on Earth are responsible for an equally sized area. Preserving Directions or providing geodesics in contrast is not important for our cause. However, most maps only cover either a subset of these features or only preserve them on a limited part on the globe. Therefore, finding an ideal map projection is not simple and will be discussed later in Section 4.2.

2.7 Replication

In general *replication* denotes the process of sharing information to ensure consistency between redundant resources. Thereby, the process pursues the goal of improving the reliability, fault-tolerance - as there is no single point of failure no more - and accessibility. We can distinguish between different types of replication. *Data replication* stores the same data on various storage devices, *computation replication* executes the same computing task several times. Computational tasks can further be divided into *replication in space* - standing for the execution on separate devices - and the *replication in time* - announcing a repeated execution on a single device.

Nr.	Projection	Name	Description
A		Azimuthal equidistant	Distances from center preserved, used for navigational purposes
B		Azimuthal equal-area	Preserves areal relationships
C		Azimuthal gnomonic	Geodesics are straight lines, strong distortions far from the center, shows less than one hemisphere
D		Azimuthal orthographic	Earth as it can be seen from outer-space
E		Azimuthal stereographic	Conformal, circle-preserving, shows at most one hemisphere
F		Conic equidistant	Constant parallel spacement leading to same scale along all meridians

Table 2.3: Overview of Projections [65]

2.7 Replication

Nr.	Projection	Name	Description
G		*Plate Carrée*	Cylindric, equidistant projection, mapping meridians and parallels to equally spaced straight lines, de-facto standard for computer applications
H		Aitoff	Modified equatorial azimuthal equidistant, stretching ellipse boundaries by 2:1
I		Bonne	Pseudoconic equal-area, parallels are equally-spaced circular arcs
J		Eckert I	Pseudocylindrical, poles have half length of Equator, meridians are straight lines, which are broken at the Equator
K		Gyoerffy E2	Pseudopolyconic projection using eight coefficients, parallel arcs show as concentric cirles resulting in minimal distortions for a region (e.g. Europe)
L		Carlos A. Furuti	Generalized, equidistant, transverse polyconic projection, poles are rotated into the equator before the projection

Table 2.4: Overview of popular Projections [65]

The terms *load balancing and backup* are often mixed up with replication. However, load balancing distributes *different* computations across several machines. Nevertheless, load balancing sometime internally uses data replication for the distribution process. A backup process saves a snapshot of data for a longer time, which remains unchanged. Replicas are rather frequently updated and not preserved for long.

Accessing a replica typically does not differ from accessing a single, not-replicated entity. The replication then is *transparent* to the user. In times of failure, the failover of replicas should remain undetectable, however sometimes users might experience delays, etc.

Regardless whether data or services are replicated, we distinguish between two processing modes: *active and passive replication*. Active replication performs the same request at any replica whereas in passive replication, each single request is processed on a single replica, only transferring the state to the others.

In the phase of distribution of updates there are two schemes that can be applied: *master-slave or multi-master*. The former denotes the existence of a so called master replica designated to process all requests. This scheme is predominant in high-availability clusters. The latter term is used if any replica may process a request. In this case, the nodes distribute the new state of the replica to the remaining replicas upon finishing the process request. Therefore, this scheme requires some form of distributed lock manager to cope with concurrent actions.

To efficiently recover from server crashes, adequate replication protocols have been proposed [66, 67]. These protocols base on transactions (a sequence of one or more operations) fulfilling the ACID properties. To distinguish between the approaches, these synchronization protocols have been classified into *pessimistic* and *optimistic* protocols.

Pessimistic protocols provide consistent data in every possible failure situation. Depending on the costs for read and write operations, we have to decide between two extreme cases. First, we can write information to all replica and then read from any (*Read One - Write All*). Or second, we can write just one replica and then read from all (*Read All - Write One*). In the latter case, we have to check the version numbers to decide on the most recent replica. Later, other replication schemes between these extremes have been developed, such as the *primary copy, majority consensus*, and *weighted voting*. The primary copy is similar to read one - write all, however not all copies are the same. At any time there is a dedicated primary copy,

2.7 Replication

which requires a lock for all operations. Thus, we can read from any copy, but have to write updates on all copies. In case of a network partitioning, an object is only accessible in the partition with its primary copy. Therefore, a crash of the primary copy must also be distinguishable from a network partitioning, making the protocol complex. To overcome these disadvantages, the concept of *voting* was introduced. In majority consensus each copy gets one vote. Locking a majority of copies (quorum) allows for a read or a write operation. As any two quorums overlap, read or write operations will always write at least one common copy. This greatly increases the availability for writing. In case of a network partitioning, the nodes in at most one partition can do read or write operations. However, in some cases e.g. a "half and half" partitioning, no partition can do any operation. The weighted voting protocol is an improvement of the majority consensus. Here, the number of votes assigned to a node can be adapted, such that reliable nodes get a higher number of votes. This increases the total availability and lowers the costs for reading.

Optimistic protocols on the other hand provide only weak consistency. Thus, short-time inconsistencies are possible. The copies then use a special function (e.g. merge) to converge to a consistent state. Therefore, these "update as soon as possible" protocols achieve a high availability.

The term replication in the "classical" sense is covered by the aspects above. It is assumed that the network is rather static, whereas Geostry deals with a highly dynamic network and thus focuses on replication schemes for a dynamic distribution of data. Furthermore, replication in Geostry is rather used for distributing highly requested information that remain unchanged. Thus, most of the aspects mentioned above do not have any effect on the replication in Geostry. In case of a failure of the initial data provider, the data will not be restored using the copies. The copies will be distributed from their hosts independent of the initial provider (see Chapter 5). As soon as the initial data provider leaves the network, we do no longer guarantee to the availability of its data.

Chapter 3

Bootstrapping in Peer-to-Peer Systems

In peer-to-peer (P2P) systems, peers form a common overlay network, either unstructured (e.g. [68, 69]) or structured (e.g. [18, 37]). Before being able to use the P2P system, e.g. to search and exchange data, a new peer must first join the overlay network. This operation is known as *bootstrapping* [70–72]. More specifically, the goal of the bootstrapping operation is to find a peer that is already a member of the overlay network. If no such network exists, the searching peer must form a new overlay network that can be discovered and joined by further peers. Without a working bootstrapping protocol, multiple isolated overlay networks may emerge, limiting the search results for all peers.

In this chapter, we present two solutions for bootstrapping in P2P systems. The first is based on the Dynamic Domain Name System (DDNS), the second uses Internet Relay Chat (IRC) to detect an existing overlay network. We describe both approaches in detail, evaluate them and discuss their strengths and shortcomings.

3.1 System Model

Before discussing the requirements of our bootstrapping approach, we describe our system model briefly.

Our system consists of a set of computers that are connected by a common communication network, e.g. the Internet. Using this network, the computers can reliably send messages to each other. We assume that a subset of these computers runs a

P2P-software. We call these computers *peers*. Peers form a connected P2P overlay network on top of the communication network. They may join and leave the overlay at any time without sending any further message. Therefore, the P2P network size varies in size from zero to all nodes of a communication network. We do not assume a specific algorithm for forming the overlay. Instead, any such algorithm can be used, e.g. [20, 37].

3.2 Requirements

In this section we describe briefly the requirements that should be fulfilled by a bootstrapping mechanism. We have presented a more detailed discussion in [70].

1. **Availability:** Availability is one of the most important properties of a bootstrapping process. Operation of the bootstrapping mechanism must be guaranteed at any time. Thus, a probabilistic approach that works only with a given probability is not sufficient. Additionally, the system should be completely decentralized to overcome the problem of a single point of failure.

2. **Automation:** To operate conveniently, the bootstrapping mechanism must work fully automated and without manual user interaction.

3. **Efficiency:** To guarantee the acceptance of a bootstrapping protocol, it has to work efficiently. Thus, a node should be able to join an overlay within a reasonable amount of time, while limiting the network traffic on the communication network to a minimum.

4. **Scalability:** Another important factor is scalability, which has to make sure that the protocol is applicable in large communication networks and in addition is able to handle a large overlay network with many peers.

3.3 Design Rationale

Before describing our approaches for bootstrapping in detail we first motivate our major design decisions. There are two classes of approaches for bootstrapping: (1) peer-based and (2) mediator-based approaches. We discuss these classes in more detail in the related work section.

Peer-based approaches try to detect peers in the overlay by contacting other peers directly. A well known example for this class are peer-caches. A peer-cache contains a list of previously known peers. When a peer wants to enter the overlay, it tries to contact a peer in its peer-cache. If it is available, the contacted peer answers and can be used as entry point into the overlay. This approach is simple and very efficient. However, it cannot guarantee that the bootstrapping succeeds, as no peer in the cache may be available or the cache may even be empty.

In contrast to this, mediator-based approaches use a well known entry point (WKEP), the mediator, to help in the discovery process. The mediator can, e.g., be a server provided by the operator of the P2P system. It manages a list of peers that are currently in the overlay and can point newly joining peers to one of them. The main challenge is to keep the mediator's data fresh and to make sure that the mediator is available. As long as this is the case, a mediator-based approach can guarantee bootstrapping. However, maintaining the mediator may consume a considerable amount of resources.

For our bootstrapping approach we combine peer-caches with a mediator acting as WKEP. First, the bootstrapping peer tries to contact any of the peers contained in its peer-cache. If this fails, it contacts the mediator and requests a currently active peer from it. This way we can take advantage of the efficiency of peer-caches and combine it with the guaranteed bootstrapping provided by the mediator. In this work we concentrate on the mediator-based part of our approach and omit the usage of peer-caches. This simplifies the presentation of our algorithms and makes them easier to understand.

Our approach requires the mediator to be highly available. One approach to achieve this is to implement the mediator as a distributed service. Clearly, the operator of a P2P system can provide this distributed service. However, doing so could result in a high overhead for the bootstrapping. Therefore, we propose to use an existing distributed Internet service as WKEP, instead of maintaining our own servers. This allows us to share the overhead of providing the distributed service with other applications that may be completely unrelated to the P2P system. To the best of our knowledge we are the first to propose using an existing distributed Internet service for bootstrapping a P2P system. A more detailed discussion of related work is given in Section 6.2.

The remaining question is, which Internet service to use for the bootstrapping process. In prior work [70] we discussed three promising services, namely (1) search engines, (2) DDNS, and (3) IRC. In this chapter, we present how to use DDNS and IRC for bootstrapping. We start by describing our approach based on DDNS in Section 3.4. After that we show an IRC-based approach in Section 3.5. We omitted implementing an approach based on search engines. The main reason for this is that search engines usually update the information they are referring to rather slowly. Thus, a new search result may become available after several hours or even days. This is too slow for an effective bootstrapping.

Note that the design of both our approaches aims at keeping the additional load for the preexisting service low. This is very important. Otherwise, if the bootstrapping induces a high level of additional load to the preexisting service, its provider will not tolerate its usage for bootstrapping.

3.4 Dynamic DNS

The Dynamic Domain Name System (DDNS) is a variant of the Domain Name System (DNS). Just like DNS it allows to map domain names to IP addresses. However, DDNS allows to change this mapping much more easily than ordinary DNS. To do so, the DDNS provider usually offers a web-based interface to change the IP address that is associated with a given name. In addition, DDNS uses very low time-to-live values to allow changing the domain name mappings dynamically. In this section, we describe a bootstrapping approach based on DDNS. We start by giving an overview of this approach and introduce the needed terminology. After that we present the details of the DDNS approach.

3.4.1 Overview

The main idea of the DDNS-based bootstrapping approach is to associate the IP address of a currently active peer with a predefined domain name. We call this peer the *bootstrapping peer* (BSP). To join the overlay, a new peer contacts the DDNS, resolves the predefined domain name (called *BS-DomainName*), and contacts the BSP. If no BSP can be resolved or the BSP does not answer, the new peer assumes that there is no overlay network present at this time and forms a new one. When the

3.4 Dynamic DNS

BSP leaves the system, another peer takes over by changing the domain name mapping to its own IP. For this approach to work we have to assure that two properties are fulfilled:

Challenge: Availability

We must guarantee that there is always a BSP present and reachable by new peers. The BSP is an ordinary peer as we do not assume the existence of super-peers. Thus, it can leave the system at any time without further notice. However, we must check the availability of the currently registered BSP regularly and must replace it if it becomes unavailable. The most straight forward way to do so is to let all other peers in the overlay try to contact the BSP periodically. Clearly, in a P2P system with many peers, this approach could easily overwhelm the BSP, as too many peers try to communicate with it. Therefore, we introduce a new peer role, so-called guardians, that take over the responsibility to check the BSP's availability. Only guardians contact the BSP periodically. If a guardian detects a missing BSP, it takes over the BSP role itself. This allows us to drastically reduce the resulting overhead for checking and keeps it at a constant level even for large peer populations. Guardians are elected from the total set of peers dynamically. If a guardian leaves the system, a new one is elected. To do so, guardians not only check the availability of the BSP but also that of other guardians. The resulting architecture of the P2P system consists of three peer groups. The BSP is responsible for letting new peers join the overlay. The guardians make sure that the BSP as well as a sufficient number of guardians is available and reelect new ones if necessary. The ordinary peers do not participate in the bootstrapping system after they joined the overlay. However, they might be contacted by a guardian at any time and made into a guardian, too.

Challenge: Efficiency

We must ensure that we do not induce too much additional load to the DDNS. Otherwise, the DDNS provider might deny our further usage of the service. Most importantly we must minimize the number of DDNS update requests, i.e., the number of requests to change the mapping between *BS-DomainName* and a new BSP's IP address. If too many update requests arrive at the DDNS in a short time, a typical DDNS installation will suspect a denial of service attack and will stop performing updates for our domain name. For our approach to be usable, we must avoid

Function	Description
DNSResolve(*domainname*)	Returns the IP address for a the given name *domainname*.
DDNSUpdate(*domainname, address*)	Updates the IP address for a given name *domainname* to the value of *address*.
CheckActive(*address*)	Checks with an overlay-based ping/pong mechanism if the address is used by an active peer.
JoinOverlay(*address*)	Enters the P2P overlay by using the given IP address.
GetGuardianCount()	Uses the BSP to retrieve the total number of active guardians.
AnnounceGuard()	Uses the BSP to announce the calling peer as a guardian.
Wait(Δt)	Waits for time Δt.
Random(*x*)	Returns a random number between 0 and x.
SendOverlay(*peer, msg*)	Sends the message *msg* to the given peer *peer*.
StartThread(*method*)	The *method* is started if it is not already running.

Table 3.1: Basic procedures used in the DDNS approach

this situation. An update request occurs in two cases. First, when a new overlay network is established and its first member becomes BSP. Second, when the current BSP leaves the system and the guardians replace it with another peer. In the first case, a problem might occur if many peers try to join a nonexisting overlay at the same time and try to become BSP at the same time. In practice, we assume this case to be rather uncommon and assume new peers to arrive in the system at random times. The second case is much more likely and we expect it to occur regularly. A problem might occur if many guardians detect the missing BSP at the same time and try to take over its role. To avoid this situation we use a randomized back-off algorithm before replacing a lost BSP.

In the following we describe our DDNS-based bootstrapping algorithm in more detail. We assume the existence of a number of basic procedures, e.g., for sending messages over the P2P overlay. We describe these procedures in Tab. 3.1.

3.4.2 Bootstrapping

When a new peer wants to join the overlay, it executes the `Bootstrapping` procedure as described in Alg. 2. The procedure is called with a single parameter, the predefined domain name (*BS-DomainName*) used for bootstrapping.

In the procedure the peer first resolves *BS-DomainName* to get the associated IP address. This IP is supposed to be the IP of the BSP. Before using the BSP to join the overlay, the peer first checks that the BSP is alive by calling the `CheckAlive` procedure. If the BSP cannot be contacted, the new peer must detect if (a) it is the first peer and should become BSP itself, or (b) the BSP is currently being replaced by another peer in the overlay. To do so, the peer waits for the maximum time needed to takeover the BSP role (Δt_{IT}) plus a randomized back-off time between 0 and ϵ. This random back-off algorithm reduces the risk that multiple peers try to update the DDNS entry at the same time. After $\Delta t_{IT} + \text{Random}(\epsilon)$ it resolves *BS-DomainName* again and repeats the test. If the BSP is still not reachable, the peer can conclude that it is the first peer, since otherwise another peer would have taken over the BSP by now. Thus, the peer becomes BSP itself by calling the `DDNSUpdate` procedure. This procedure maps *BS-DomainName* to the peer's IP address.

Algorithm 2 The main DDNS bootstrapping procedure
1: **procedure** Bootstrapping(*BS-DomainName*)
2:    // *LocalIP* is the local IP-Address
3:    *IP* := DNSResolve(*BS-DomainName*);
4:    **if** CheckActive(*IP*) **then**
5:      JoinOverlay(*IP*);
6:      CheckBecomeGuardian();
7:    **else**
8:      Wait($\Delta t_{IT} + \text{Random}(\epsilon)$);
9:      *IP* := DNSResolve(*BS-DomainName*);
10:      **if** CheckActive(*IP*) **then**
11:        JoinOverlay(*IP*);
12:        CheckBecomeGuardian();
13:      **else**
14:        DDNSUpdate(*BS-DomainName*, *LocalIP*);
15:      **end if**
16:    **end if**

Note that this approach cannot guarantee that only exactly one peer assumes to be BSP. However, this does not do any harm, because the DDNS entry unambiguously determines the current BSP.

After successfully joining the P2P overlay network every peer (except the BSP) checks if it should become a guardian peer by calling the `CheckBecomeGuardian` procedure (see Alg. 3).

Algorithm 3 Checking whether to become a guardian

1: **procedure** CheckBecomeGuardian()
2:   **if** GetGuardiansCount() < GuardThreshold **then**
3:     Wait(Random(Δt_G + Random(ϵ)));
4:     **if** GetGuardianCount() < GuardThreshold **then**
5:       StartThread(BSPWatchdog());
6:       StartThread(GuardWatchdog());
7:       AnnounceGuard();
8:     **end if**
9:   **end if**

It first checks if there are enough guardian peers active. If there are too few guardian peers active (i.e. fewer than *GuardThreshold*) the peer must wait for some randomized time Δt_G + Random(ϵ). This waiting time is needed to prevent situations where many peers become guardians at the same time. If the number of active guardian peers is still below the threshold after the second check, the peer must become a guardian peer itself.

A guardian peer has two responsibilities. First, it must regularly check if the BSP is still active (`BSPWatchdog`). If not, it tries to become BSP itself. Secondly, a guardian is responsible for regularly checking if there are enough other guardian peers active, in case one of them leaves the overlay (`GuardWatchdog`). Note that this check is done in addition to the check done by new peers. When a peer becomes a guardian it announces this to the BSP by using the `AnnounceGuard` procedure. This allows the BSP to keep track of the current number of active guardians and to realize the `GetGuardianCount` procedure.

3.4.3 Maintenance

In the following we describe the two watchdog procedures used by guardian peers. We start with `BSPWatchdog`. After that we describe `GuardWatchdog`.

As already mentioned, a responsibility of a guardian peer is to check whether the BSP is still active. This is achieved by using the `BSPWatchdog` procedure given in Algorithm 4.

3.4 Dynamic DNS

Algorithm 4 Checking the bootstrap peer
1: **procedure** BSPWatchdog()
2: **while true do**
3:    $IP := \text{DNSResolve}(BS\text{-}DomainName)$;
4:    **if not** CheckActive(IP) **then**
5:       Wait(Random(Δt_T + Random(ϵ)));
6:       $IP := \text{DNSResolve}(BS\text{-}DomainName)$;
7:       **if not** CheckActive(IP) **then**
8:          DDNSUpdate($BS\text{-}DomainName$, $LocalIP$);
9:          **return**
10:       **end if**
11:    **end if**
12:    Wait(Δt_{TI});
13: **end while**

It runs an endless loop in which the guardian peer regularly checks if the BSP is still active. If this is the case, the peer waits for the interval time Δt_{TI} before checking again. Otherwise, the guardian peer waits for the randomized time Δt_T+Random(ϵ). This waiting time is needed to prevent multiple takeovers of the domain name *BS-DomainName*, effectively preventing update bursts. After waiting for the back-off time, the peer checks a second time. If no new BSP is detected, it takes over the BSP role itself. If a guardian becomes the BSP, it exits the BSP watchdog – since there is no need to check itself.

In addition to the `BSPWatchdog` procedure, each guardian executes the `GuardWatchdog` procedure (see Alg. 5). Just like `BSPWatchdog`, this procedure runs in an endless loop.

Algorithm 5 Checking the number of active guardians
1: **procedure** GuardWatchdog()
2: **while true do**
3:    **if** GetGuardiansCount() < *GuardThreshold* **then**
4:       Wait(Random(Δt_G + Random(ϵ)));
5:       **if** GetGuardianCount() < *GuardThreshold* **then**
6:          SendOverlay(*SomeActivePeer*, "BecomeGuard");
7:       **end if**
8:    **end if**
9:    Wait(Δt_{GI});
10: **end while**

First, it checks if there are enough active guardians, i.e., more than *GuardThreshold*. If this is the case, the guardian waits for a time Δt_{GI} and starts over. Otherwise, one or more guardians have left the overlay since the last check and must be replaced by new guardians. To achieve this, the guardian chooses an arbitrary peer in the overlay and sends an invitation message to it. Clearly, this peer must not be the BSP or a guardian already. After receiving the invitation, the peer becomes a new guardian. Again, this approach can lead to multiple guardians inviting new peers at the same time, resulting in too many guardians. To reduce this effect, we use another randomized back-off time $\Delta t_G + \text{Random}(\epsilon)$. Before inviting a peer, the guardian waits for the back-off time and checks again. The invitation is sent only if there are still too few guardians.

3.5 Internet Relay Chat

The Internet Relay Chat (IRC) [73] is one of the oldest decentralized services on the Internet. All participating servers are interconnected, thus allowing a client to connect to any of the servers while being able to communicate with any other client, even if the client is connected to another server. When IRC was introduced there was essentially one big IRC network. However, this network grew so fast that in about 1996 the one big IRC network was split in multiple smaller networks. Today many thousands of IRC networks coexist in the Internet, while the biggest ones are QuakeNet, EFnet, IRCNet and Undernet. Nodes that connect to one of those networks communicate with nodes from the same IRC network only.

With its highly decentralized, almost non-killable architecture, the IRC service is a good choice for bootstrapping a P2P network. Actually, IRC was already used in Gnutella to find out about other peers [3], but this approach required the user to take some manual actions. We envision a direct, fully-automated use of the IRC service by the peers of the P2P network without any further user interaction. The user does not have to bother with the bootstrapping itself - it simply connects.

The founder of an overlay selects one of the larger IRC networks and has new nodes connect to one of the servers of this specific network. A list of suitable IRC servers is provided with the client software or listed on the project website. The new client then implements the following steps (see Algorithm 6) for a successful bootstrapping using the procedures listed in Tab 3.2.

3.5 Internet Relay Chat

Function	Description
Connect(*IRCServer*)	Returns true if link establishment successful.
Join(*IRCChannel*)	Returns true if channel entry successful.
Leave(*IRCChannel*)	Leaves the specified IRC channel.
JoinOverlay(*address*)	Enters the P2P overlay using the given IP address.
GetBSPCount()	Uses the IRC *ListMsg* to determine the number of active BSPs.
SetNick(*Name*)	Set the peer's nickname to $Name \in \{Peer, BSP\}$.
Wait(Δt)	Waits for time Δt.
SendChannel(*msg*)	Sends the message *msg* into the IRC channel.
SendOverlay(*peer, msg*)	Sends the message *msg* to the given peer *peer*.

Table 3.2: Basic procedures used in the IRC approach

3.5.1 Bootstrapping Phase

After a node has successfully connected to an arbitrary *IRC server* of the same network, it enters a well-known chat room, a so-called *channel*. The peer then chooses an ID (here: nick), which comprises of an identifier for the overlay (e.g. 'peer') and a random number. Using this nick, the peer calls the Join procedure and thus receives a list of all members, which are currently in the channel. Within this list, the node then searches for a bootstrap peer by checking for an appropriate nick (e.g. *'bootstrapPeer < id >'*). In case several peers enter the channel simultaneously the channel will contain peers and BSPs. However, peers will not be used for bootstrapping other peers as they do not have sufficient information yet. Entering a channel thus leads to the following two cases:

No Bootstrap Peer in Channel

If the member list does not contain a bootstrap peer the peer has no chance to learn about other peers from the overlay. Thus, the node becomes a bootstrap peer itself and therefore calls SetNick to change its nick from *'peer < id >'* to *'bootstrapPeer < id >'*. The bootstrapping phase ends in that case, though the BSP is not yet aware of other nodes. This situation only occurs when a new overlay is established. Once new peers enter the channel, the BSP is able to provide them with its own IP address.

Bootstrap Peer available

In case the node has found a bootstrap peer in the current member list, it waits for a random time $t_{WBQ}+\text{Random}(\epsilon)$ before querying the bootstrap peer (`SendChannel`). The random timespan allows for flash crowds to enter the channel simultaneously. Without it, the bootstrapping would still work, the amount of queries to the BSP would just be elevated. Eventually, one node will ask the bootstrap node for his IP address. As the IRC implements an application multicast, the answer (the question as well) is heard by all nodes in the channel. Thus, all other nodes waiting for an address are served as well and do not have to ask separately. This approach is not only efficient, but as well necessary as most IRC servers have a strict limit on how many concurrent messages they allow within a certain time interval.

Algorithm 6 IRC Bootstrapping in general

1: **procedure** Bootstrap(*IRCServer, bootstrap-channel*)
2:   Connect(*IRCServer*)
3:   Join(*bootstrap-channel*)
4:   Wait($\Delta(t_{WBQ}) + \text{Random}(\epsilon)$)
5:   SendChannel("RequestActivePeer")
6:   **if** JoinOverlay(*ActivePeer.IP*) **then**
7:     Leave(*Channel*)
8:   **else**
9:     BecomeBSP()
10:   **end if**

3.5.2 Joining the Overlay

After the bootstrapping phase, the peer enters the overlay using the IP address of a BSP which it was given before (`JoinOverlay`). Therefore, it then sends a request to the BSP outside the channel using direct communication. Doing so does not impose any load on the IRC service provider. The BSP then sends all information necessary to enter the overlay. Once the peer successfully connects with the overlay it leaves the IRC channel shortly after. As we have to keep the communication in the channel minimal, only BSPs remain in the channel. In case there are enough BSPs new peers will leave the channel as soon as they have joined the overlay. If a node cannot connect to the overlay network within a given time interval, it chooses another bootstrapping node and reruns the bootstrapping phase until it eventually succeeds.

3.5.3 At Runtime

Bootstrap peers have a special task, as they have to guarantee a successful bootstrap at all times. Through the `Self-Healing` procedure, they discover (see `GetBSPCount`) when the amount of bootstrap peers drops under a specified *BSPThreshold*. In this event, the node will wait a random timespan until it will recheck whether the situation has improved through actions of another BSP. If not, the bootstrap node will start to invite peers out of its own peer cache and have them join the channel and thus, become bootstrap peers, too (see `SendOverlay`). Similar to the DDNS approach random delays have to be introduced before sending invitations or the amount of BSPs in the channel may grow unnecessarily.

Upon the request of becoming a bootstrap peer, the node, which is still in the channel, simply changes its nick to resemble its new role. In the more likely case that the node receiving the invitation is currently not in the channel, it has to connect to the IRC network, enter the channel of the overlay and assign itself an appropriate nick. In doing so, the approach is able to deal with the passive leaving of nodes.

Algorithm 7 Self-Healing Mechanisms in the IRC
1: **procedure** SelfHealing
2: **if** Peer.role == BSP **then**
3:    **while** GetBSPCount() < BSPThreshold **do**
4:       Wait(Δt_{SH} + Random(ϵ));
5:       SendOverlay(*SomeActivePeer*, "BecomeBSP");
6:    **end while**
7: **end if**

3.5.4 Leaving

The active leaving process is comparably simple. A regular peer may simply leave the overlay without any further procedures. Bootstrap peers have to check whether the number of their kind is still above the *BSPThreshold*. If that's the case, the peer may leave the channel and the overlay. In the other case, the bootstrap peer has to invite a node out of its own peer cache to take its place. Here as well, the node keeps sending invitations until the condition is satisfied.

3.6 Evaluation

In this evaluation we focus on the bootstrapping process itself, not on a specific peer-to-peer protocol. Thus, we only consider messages that are necessary to bootstrap or pose a load on a participating peer. Messages containing node caches, ping/pong messages for keeping the neighborhood list accurate etc. are left aside therefore.

To fortify the practicability of our approaches we implemented two prototypes using C#. In our simulations we examined the traffic necessary to provide a successful bootstrapping for both the DDNS and the IRC approach. Therefore, we created a set of scenarios with different join and leave parameters as follows.

Scenario 1: To model a realistic behavior of peer arrival and leaving we chose to use Markov birth and death processes [74]. As the birth and death of a process are independent from previous events, we set the birth rates $\lambda_0 = \lambda_1 = ... = \lambda_n = 0.8$ respectively the death rates $\mu_0 = \mu_1 = ... = \mu_n = 0.81$ equal for all nodes of the Markov chain. The total runtime for the simulation was one hour with an event (birth or death) taking place every 10 sec.

Scenario 2: On the other hand, we want to make sure that our approaches cope with a steady rise of nodes as well. In the DDNS approach we therefore randomly generated between 1 and 5 nodes every 5 seconds until we reach the desired amount. Each node comes with a lifetime between 4 and 6 minutes after which it will leave without sending further messages. Each node leaving the network is replaced within the next 5 seconds the latest, thus keeping the overall amount on the desired value. We started with 10 nodes in Step 1 and increased the amount of nodes in each step by 10 until a total of 50 nodes in Step 5. Each of the steps lasted for 30 minutes and got repeated 5 times, leading to an overall simulation time of 12,5 hours. For the IRC approach we used the identical parameters except for the stepping. We increased the node amount from 1 to 50 within a 10 minute period and picked an exemplary gradient for Fig. 3.2(b).

The node amounts given in this scenario only cover the nodes, that have joined the overlay from that point on. Assuming that we want to consider all participating nodes during the overall simulation runtime, we have to include the nodes that have left the bootstrapping aid and "only" remain in the overlay. With a maximum lifetime of 6 minutes, we have bootstrapped at least 250 nodes within the first 30

3.6 Evaluation

minutes. This should point out, that the numbers of peers in the evaluation may be small, but cannot be associated directly with the amount of peers in the overlay.

3.6.1 DDNS

Each approach uses a different set of messages due to the underlying infrastructure. For the DDNS evaluation, we considered the following message types:

- `UpdateDomain`: messages that are used to tell the DDNS server that a new guardian has become bootstrap peer
- `GetAddress`: resolves the domain and thus informs the requesting peer about the current bootstrap peer
- `Ping/Pong`: these messages are used by the guardians to check the liveliness of the bootstrap peer

The update domain messages have to stay low. That is at most one message per minute. Otherwise most DDNS providers (e.g. dyndns.com) will disable the update function and lock the domain for at least some time. Each peer willing to enter the overlay will contact the DDNS server using a `GetAddress` message. Thus, the amount of messages will increase with growing networks. However, as DDNS is scalable due to its complex hierarchy, these messages will be compensated and effect neither the DDNS provider nor the bootstrap peer. Yet, the bootstrap peer has to cope with the ping messages sent by the guardians. As the amount of guardians varies only slightly regardless of the amount of peers in the overlay, this amount stays constantly low.

Results:

At first, we consider the load on the DDNS server using Scenario 1. In Figure 3.1(a) we analyze the messages arriving at the DDNS server: the `GetAddress` and `UpdateDomain` messages. The amount of `GetAddress` messages is dependent on the amount of nodes requesting a name resolution. However, this name resolution does not put any load on the DDNS server, but uses the DNS protocol. The DNS protocol relies on a hierarchical architecture with caching servers and thus isolates this traffic from the DDNS provider. The `UpdateDomain` messages are the ones that are really important. Too many messages of this kind may bring the service provider to close this account and the corresponding domain. However, we can see that only very few updates occur. This is due to a high lifetime of the bootstrapping peers and the guardian concept. To verify that availability of the BSP, the guardians exchange Ping/Pong messages with it. A high amount of messages may stress the BSP and render it unusable. As the number of guardians stays constant, the amount of messages sent and the load on the BSP stays constant as well (see Figure 3.1(b)).

In Figure 3.1(c) we can see the behavior of the participating peers using Scenario 2. We separated the measurement into 5 steps with each one lasting for 30 minutes. The values for the various message types in each step are summed up and compared. It shows that increasing the numbers of participants only has minimal effect on the amount of messages being sent. We see that the amount of Ping/Pong messages stays constant. This is again due to the constant amount of guardians in the network. The number of GetAddress messages stays rather constant as well. As mentioned before, this is not our primary objective since the DDNS architecture takes care of name resolutions. In this scenario there are more domain updates (see UpdateDomain messages) as the lifetime of a bootstrap peer is limited to a maximum of 6 minutes. Nevertheless, the guardians absorb the messages resulting in the change of bootstrap peers and thereby keep the overall message count for the DDNS constantly low.

3.6.2 IRC

Using the IRC approach fewer messages have to be sent due to the multicast nature of the IRC channel. Therefore, we only have to consider the following message types:

- ChannelMessages: whenever a node enters the channel it asks for an IP and receives an answer

- Invitations: are sent if there are not enough bootstrap peers in the channel at the moment

Most IRC server implementations pose a tight limit on the amount of messages being sent in the channel. This feature should suppress message flooding and is usually set to 10 messages / second. If a node sends more messages it will be kicked from the channel and in some cases even banned from the IRC server. In case a bootstrap peer leaves the channel, we have to ensure that our protocol is still working. Thus,

3.6 Evaluation

we have the other bootstrapping peers send an invitation to peers of the overlay using out-of-channel communication. As these messages are not sent through the IRC channel they do not put any load on the IRC provider.

Results: As we use several bootstrap peers in the channel the load on each one stays low as there are no periodic messages, that have to be sent. Rather a single invitation per missing bootstrap peer is sent to a peer from the overlay network (see Figure 3.2). The amount of messages in the channel depends on the node arrival frequency. The more nodes arrive within a short time interval the more requests are sent. The time between joining a channel and sending a request for an IP plus the fact that channel messages are broadcasted allows for a constantly low message rate. In neither scenario the total message rate exceeds 16 messages / minute, which is far below the typical limitations of 10 messages / second / host. Even in the case of a steadily growing node amount (Figure 3.2(b)) the amount of bootstrap peers in the overlay stays constant.

3.6.3 Open Issues

In this work, we focus more on the technical feasibility than on security aspects. One of the major weaknesses of the DDNS approach is the fact that each domain is accessible via a password only. A malicious node could change this password and thereby hinder all nodes to update their DDNS entries with their most recent IP addresses. Nodes will then either receive node caches with addresses from malicious respectively fake nodes or not receive a node cache at all. However, this approach does not differ from a major authority's effort to cut off file-sharing by providing their own supernodes in KaZaA. Furthermore, in case the bootstrap peer changes frequently due to log-offs, additional pauses have to be introduced. Otherwise, the DDNS server would receive too many updates and lock the account for this subdomain.

In the IRC approach, channels may be protected through a password, but do not necessarily need one. A general idea on how to overcome this problem can be found in our earlier work [75]. If the password is omitted everyone can join the channel and look for a bootstrap peer. The major issue in the IRC is the message count. As most IRC server implementations only allow for a low amount of messages (usually around 10 msg/sec), certain precautions have to be taken. We cannot limit the

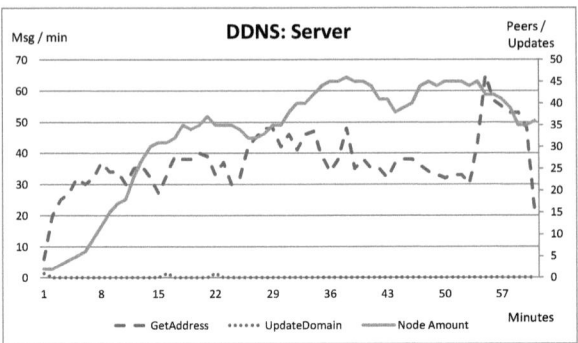

(a) DDNS Server Load

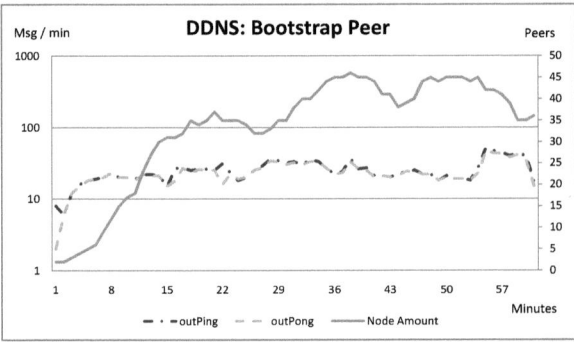

(b) Load on Bootstrap Peer using DDNS

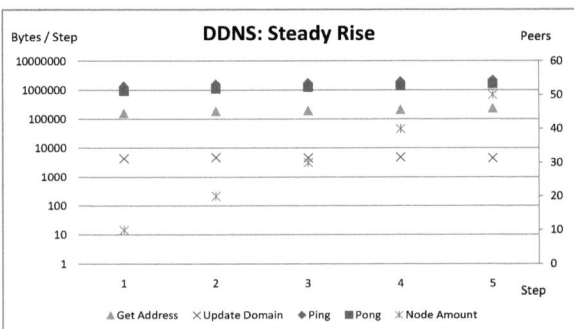

(c) DDNS Behavior under a steady rise

Figure 3.1: Evaluations on DDNS

3.7 Summary

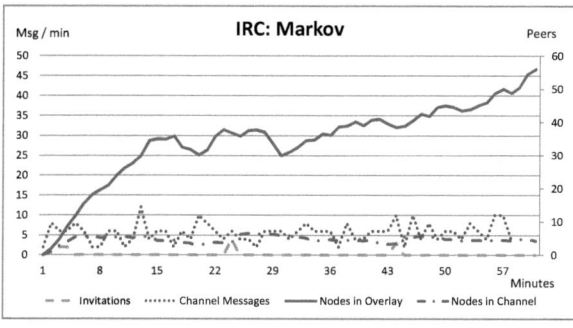

(a) IRC Load using Markov

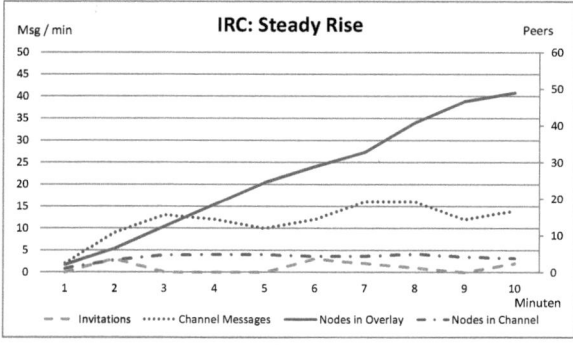

(b) IRC Behavior under a steady rise

Figure 3.2: Evaluations on IRC

amount of nodes entering the channel. However, due to the broadcast nature of a channel not all nodes have to send a request. With our protocol nodes enter the channel and wait for a short time. As the reply is heard by everyone in the channel all nodes that have entered after the first node will be able to bootstrap as well.

3.7 Summary

Solving the bootstrapping problem is a challenging task. As we will see later in this work, none of the existing approaches satisfies all the requirements for an efficient and robust bootstrapping protocol. In this chapter, we presented two approaches offering a solution for this challenge. We use existing Internet services as a fallback whenever the peer-based approach fails. These services are distributed and therefore have a high availability adding robustness to our approaches. Through the evaluation we have shown that our protocols can be used for the bootstrapping while putting a constantly low load on the underlying infrastructure only.

In the case of DDNS, we showed that it is very *efficient*, since a node normally only needs to perform a single DNS request to detect an existing peer. Furthermore, it is *robust against failure*, as leaving peers are detected and others take their place. Security appliances also pose no problem as DNS can be used behind firewalls and NAT-routers. In addition, the approach is highly *scalable* as the number of guardians is independent from the participating nodes. The only data the user has to enter manually is the domain, which is used for the then *automated* bootstrapping. Unfortunately, users have to be aware of a common password to update the DDNS entry. If this password is changed, future updates will not be possible.

The IRC-based approach features the same advantages as the one using the DDNS. It works *efficiently*, since it uses only few resources on the host-service and the *automated* operation of joining the overlay is just a matter of trying nodes from the peer cache and additionally (in the unsuccessful case) a connection to an IRC server. To hinder the bootstrapping an ordinary attacker would have to shut down potentially thousands of IRC servers. Hence, this approach fulfills our *availability* requirement. As all peers immediately leave the IRC-channel after successfully bootstrapping, *scalability* poses no problem as well.

One challenge remains, as an IRC operator could ban users or protect a channel to complicate the bootstrapping. To counter this, additional measures are necessary, e.g. random user names and "hot swapping" the channel at runtime. Furthermore, we want to increase the robustness of both our approaches and make them more difficult to shutdown. At the moment, our prototype already supports the use of several subdomains (e.g. *peer1...peerX.myp2pnetwork.ddnsprovider.net*). Currently we are working on enhancing our IRC protocol to match the robustness of the enhanced DDNS protocol. Therefore, we are expanding the prototype with the IRC equivalent of subdomains and have it use multiple IRC channels simultaneously.

Special care has to be taken with these protocols as they can easily be abused for controlling large amounts of hacked computers, e.g. bot-nets [76, 77]. Currently bot-nets rely on fast flux networks, which require a very cooperative DDNS server. In contrast, our approach is able to work within standard parameters of the service providers, i.e. DDNS and IRC.

Chapter 4

Spatial Queries

In this chapter, we illustrate how to support spatial queries. As shown in Section 2.4.2, we therefore need to facilitate position queries, neighborhood queries and region queries. We assume that the participants of our overlay are equipped with a GPS-device or another means of positioning gadget and that we mainly deal with stationary peers. Additionally, we assume the users have access to a geo-tool offering GPS coordinates for the world. Thus, every user can compute the appropriate node ID to participate in our overlay network in respect to a given location by applying our space-filling curve layout. Using this node ID, we build a routing algorithm that allows for finding a peer geographically-close to a specific location, thus solving the problem of answering position queries. Enabling the other two types of spatial queries is more challenging and is explained in the sections thereafter.

4.1 Location-based P2P & Locality

Location-based systems have become more and more popular recently as they can be used for many different scenarios. However, there are still some challenges when using peer-to-peer systems as an overlay network for location-based applications. We relate a location to a specific entity (person, object, ...), which is located somewhere on this planet. Therefore, the appropriate coordinates are 2- or even 3-dimensional (latitude, longitude and altitude respectively). Figure 4.1(a) illustrates such a 2-dimensional representation of our planet. Modern P2P systems however use a ring structure to organize themselves, a node solely knows its neighbors in the circular ID space (1-dimensional) as shown in Figure 4.1(b). To counter this problem, we need a dimension reduction to map the multi-dimensional data (for the location) onto the ring (for the nodes to store).

Locality vs. Willingness

In addition, we want to optimize our P2P system towards locality. Due to latency and security issues it would be best to store information concerning a certain location on a computer close to it. However, there is also a social component that plays an important role. Participants of overlays implicitly agree to host "foreign" data. In our geographic-related scenario, this would mean that for instance users in New York might have to store data about Moscow. As there is usually no real benefit in doing so, users tend to retrieve information when they need it and then leave the overlay afterwards without providing resources to the other participants. Many P2P networks share this problem, which is commonly known as the free-rider [78] problem. We believe, that by storing data about geographically-close locations we can soften this problem.

To implement locality, the peers in our system have to identify their own location and the location to which the context-information is relevant. Thus, we can ensure that the opening hours of the Berlin Pergamon Museum are stored on a peer in Berlin and not in Tokyo. To solve these two major problems we present an algorithm, which is based on Pastry [37]. By applying space-filling curves (SFC) it optimizes the data distribution for a close relation between the location the information is about and the location the data is actually stored at. With our approach we want to extend the functionality of the Nexus project [79][80][7] through the use of P2P technology. Throughout this chapter, we present a method for implementing spatial queries in a geographically optimized P2P network and the implicated challenges.

4.2 World Partitioning

Our algorithm bases upon Pastry, which is organized in a ring structure. In plain Pastry each peer is assigned a unique ID through the use of a hash-function over the IP address. To answer a query the according key ID is calculated and sent to the node with the ID "closest" to it (prefix routing). However, the method for assigning IDs to nodes as used in Pastry is sub-optimal for the use in our scenario. It uses

4.2 World Partitioning

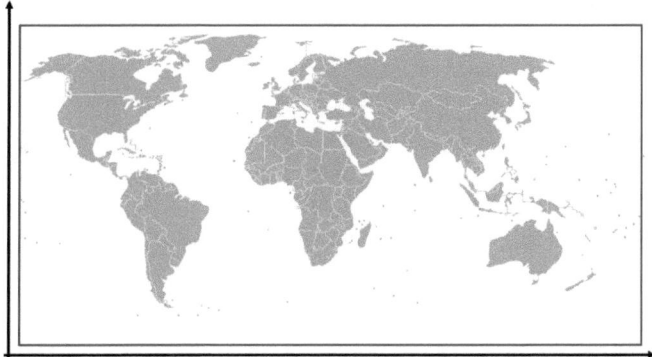

(a) 2-dimensional map of Earth [81]

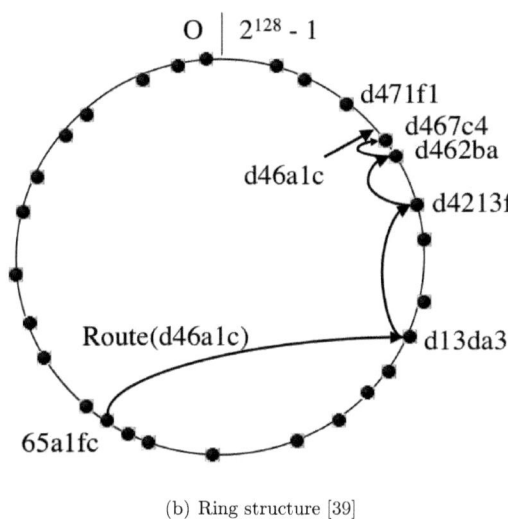

(b) Ring structure [39]

Figure 4.1: Mapping 2-dimensional coordinates on a 1-dimensional ring

a hash function to calculate the node ID, which results in the fact that nodes with adjacent node IDs may be diverse in geography. This assignment scheme thus leads to a low locality which is highly undesirable in our scenario, as queries might have to travel long distances. In contrast, our algorithm optimizes the location where data is stored.

To achieve our goal of assigning an ID corresponding to the location of the node, we divide the world into equally-sized zones [82]. For the remainder of the chapter we regard the world as a 2-dimensional quadratic map (see Figure 4.2). Still, it poses no problem to enhance our model to support a third dimension (additional bits are concatenated with the IDs). Each zone then represents the smallest area a single node can be responsible for. The more zones, the more nodes can be supported. We believe using 56 bit for encoding the node ID will be sufficient for most applications as a single zone then covers less than $0,007 m^2$. Upon booting a node determines its geographical position, the zone it is in and thereupon calculates its node ID to participate in the P2P ring. To cope with imprecision of positioning devices and the fact that several devices may exist at the same spot (e.g. in a tall building), we add 8 additional random bits to the 56 bit key, such that the overall key length sums up to 64 bits. In the unlikely case, that a node wants to choose the node ID of an already existing peer, this behavior is detected during the bootstrapping phase and can be easily corrected by choosing a new random identifier. Thus, the additional bits do not increase the spatial resolution, but rather add to the total amount of nodes supported.

Zone Indexing

Henceforward, we are able to assign an ID to each zone. Since, we do want to implement locality of data, adjacent zones should share a similar ID as in our scenario this also implies geographical-proximity. Thus, the ultimate challenge is to have a minimum difference between actual geographic distance and the distance in ID space for all zones. In terms of nodes of peer-to-peer network we want to make sure that if the geographic distance between two random nodes is small, their node IDs will be numerically close, too. Thereby, we limit the distance messages have to travel. However, designing a space-filling curve C, such that all points close in multi-dimensional space $[N]^m$ are close along the curve is impossible. The authors of [83] have shown that "there will always be at least one pair of close points in $[N]^m$ that are very far apart along C". This provides several methods on how to calculate

4.2 World Partitioning

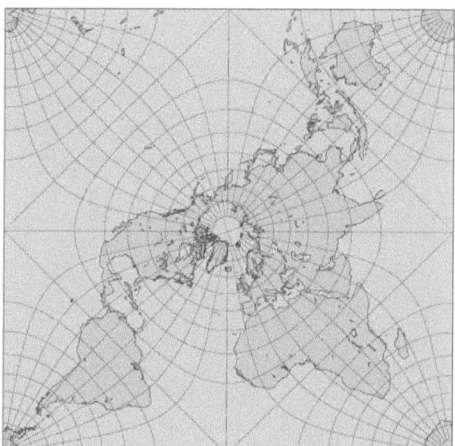

Figure 4.2: 2D World Model (Map projection after Peirce [60])

the node ID. In [84] the author has shown that space-filling curves surpass other mappings in most cases though. Yet, [83] proved that it is impossible to create a SFC, such that all points close in the multi-dimensional space are close on the curve, too. Therefore, we compare different curves by identifying their characteristics and conclude their usefulness in our scenario. In contrast to other work [85][86] we investigate locality in small-world population scenarios, too.

Peirce Projection

For the projection in Fig. 4.2 we have chosen to use the transverse case of the *Guyou* projection, also known as *Peirce* or *Quincuncial* projection [87], which was developed by Charles Sanders Peirce in 1879. Though this projection is used rather seldom, it was applied for world-maps of air routes by the U.S. Coast and Geodetic Survey [88] and spherical panoramas where it can present the entire sphere with most areas being recognizable [89].

In contrast to Guyou which has an equatorial aspect, Peirce has a polar aspect and is therefore often classified as an azimuthal projection. The term "quincuncial" derives from a whole-Earth projection into a square consisting of a central diamond square and four corner one-fourth squares. The resulting five regions are responsible for the latinized name "quincuncial". The scale is not true anywhere, its worse effects are visible at the four "corners" of the projection, where the scale is elongated. Additionally the scale is compressed at the poles. However, in regard to the entire map the overall scale deviation using the Peirce projection is very low (around 9% in contrast to Mercator with 13% or to Stereographic with 50%) [90]. Furthermore, the majority of the population does not live at the poles, but rather on the other continents where the distances are preserved far better. The Peirce projection is also conformal (except for the "corners") and thus locally preserves angles. To avoid Brazil being "cut-off" at two inner squares, we rotate Earth by 20°. Through the square form of the projection, we can easily apply space-filling curves onto it as they too progress quadratically. For these reasons, we have concluded that the Peirce projection is suited best in our scenario.

4.3 Space-Filling Curves

G. Cantor proved that it is possible to bijectively map the interval $I = [0, 1]$ onto the space $\Omega = [0, 1]^d ; d \in N$ [55]. G. Peano then defined, that a space-filling curve $f : I \longmapsto \Omega \subset \mathbb{R}^d$ is surjective and Ω is positive in $\mathbb{R}^d$. This definition led to the development of several curves, which can be distinguished by their level of locality. Locality indicates the relationship of the distance of two points $p1, p2 \in I$ on the SFC and its image $f(p1), f(p2) \in \Omega$ in the multi-dimensional space. We search a curve with good locality properties or more precisely: $p1 \approx p2 \Leftrightarrow f(p1) \approx f(p2)$.

For the remainder of the chapter, we state, that we solely regard discretizations of the curves, as we use them for assigning IDs to nodes only. We cannot determine the locality of a curve by exclusively analyzing its geometric representation. However, it is obvious that long edges worsen locality, as there is larger difference in geography and only a minimal difference in ID space, which for example is the problem of the trivial S-shaped curve. In the following, we compare a selection of space-filling curves, that promise good locality. Several sources present further SFCs [55][59], however, most curves show a certain level of similarity or are not suited for our purpose.

4.3 Space-Filling Curves

4.3.1 S-shaped Curve

The simplest way to map an index curve onto an area is to superimpose the curve in an s-shaped way. This approach is not very promising, as the expected error is elevated. This is due to the fact that geographically close nodes may have a large discrepancy in their node IDs. For example, the first element of the first two rows are geographically close, but their node IDs differ by two times the edge length of the area as can be seen in Figure 4.3.

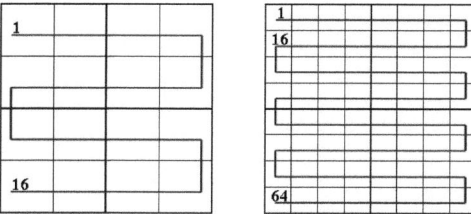

Figure 4.3: Trivial S-shaped Curve

4.3.2 Lebesgue

One of the simpler space-filling curves is described by the standard *Lebesgue Curve* [55] (also known as Z-order curve). It allows for an easy conversion from the indices in the 2-dimensional matrix to the 1-dimensional index along the curve, which makes it extremely attractive for the use in our scenario. The index of a point p is calculated as follows: $x = (x_0 x_1 ... x_n), y = (y_0 y_1 ... y_n) \rightarrow P_{index} = y_0 x_0 y_1 x_1 ... y_n x_n$

Figure 4.4 shows that the resulting curve is self-avoiding, but contains some long edges, which is not optimal for our purpose.

4.3.3 Peano

Peano presented the first curve fulfilling the definition 2.2. The partitioning of that curve differs from all other well-known SFC. On each partitioning step, each zone is split into three slices in each dimension. Therefore, the unit square is divided into nine zones in the first step. The curve then follows the initial mapping as in Figure 4.5 (left image). The distances between two adjacent nodes on the curve is

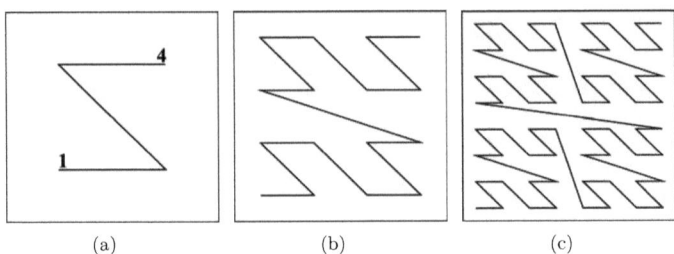

Figure 4.4: Lebesgue Curve (Order 1-3)

homogeneous, thus the curve is often applied in other research areas, such as cache-optimizations [91]. [55] gives further details as well as an analytical description of the curve.

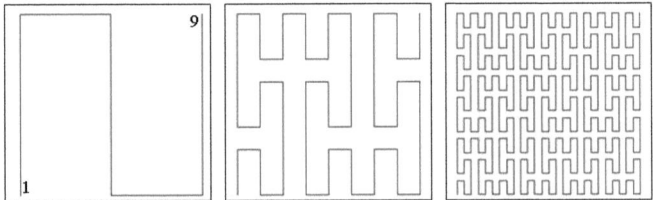

Figure 4.5: Peano Curve (Order 1-3)

4.3.4 Hilbert

Shortly after Peano presented his SFC, David Hilbert proposed another important curve. In the area of mesh-indexing the authors of [85] could prove that in the worst case scenario the Hilbert curve provided best geometric locality properties. Its geometric construction starts with the basic "u"-form (left image of Figure 4.6). The order-2 curve is then generated by shrinking its size such that four copies can be placed on the grid. While the position of the upper two curves matches their final orientation, the lower curves have to be rotated according to their position on the unit square (see middle image of Figure 4.6). Lastly, the ends facing each other have to be connected, forming the continuous curve. For further orders this procedure is applied recursively to all partial squares. We will later give further examples on how to exploit the self-similarity of the Hilbert SFC to allow for an easy construction (see Section 4.6).

4.4 Evaluation

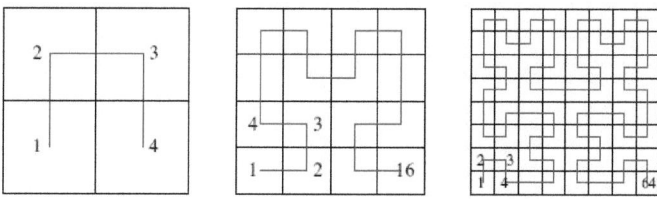

Figure 4.6: Hilbert Curve (Order 1-3)

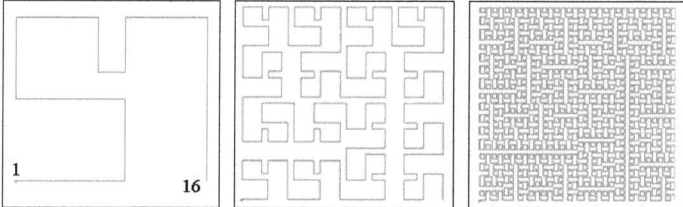

Figure 4.7: Fass II Curve (Order 1-3)

4.3.5 Fass II

Fass is an acronym for space-filling, self-avoiding, simple and self-similar curves. Besides the Hilbert and Peano curve we analyze another interesting Fass curve [59], basing on the following Lindenmayer [92][93] parameters:
$Angle = 90°$, $Axiom = -L$, $Rules = \{$
$L \rightarrow LFLF + RFR + FLFL - FRF - LFL - FR + F + RF - LFL - FRFRFR+,$
$R \rightarrow -LFLFLF + RFR + FL - F - LF + RFR + FLF + RFRF - LFL - FRFR\}.$
Similar rules are used in Turtle Graphics [94], where a "plus" indicates a turn by 90 degrees to the left ("minus" to the right) and an "F" marks the next point or zone in our scenario. Starting with the axiom (initial value), the next order curve is generated by replacing the "L" and "R" according to the rules. The resulting curve resembles the digit four, as can be seen in Figure 4.7.

4.4 Evaluation

In this section, we identify the suitability of the curves for the use in our scenario. Therefore, we conducted several tests, measuring the average error distribution, analyzing the locality in dense and sparse populated worlds and testing the behavior in small-world networks.

4.4.1 Mean Error Rate

The mean error rate (MER) reflects the average deviation of the geographic coordinates and the assigned IDs rather than an actual error. Even in the "error" case we will still find a node that can forward the query to the target node, certain factors (e.g. latency) however may be worse.

For setup, we assume to have a node in each zone, being assigned an ID as the curve passes by. We then compare each node with every other node and calculate the difference in geometric and ID space. As the curves use different partitioning processes (Peano generates 9 squares whereas some others use 4) we cannot calculate the sum of all these differences for comparison. Therefore, we devise the MER independent of the zone count as we normalize the ID difference and the euclidean distance (Δgeo). We then sum up all these values and normalize this result to devise the MER for every curve as in Eq. 4.1.

$$MER_{curve} = \sum_{i=1}^{n} \frac{\sum_{j=1, j \neq i}^{n} \left| \frac{|i-j|}{n} - \frac{|\Delta geo(i,j)|}{\sqrt{2}n} \right|}{n} \quad (4.1)$$

Figure 4.8 illustrates the error distribution for the complete unit square. The darker the zone, the higher its mean error.

The following Table 4.1 shows the different MERs per curve. It shows that the more complex space-filling curves are more efficient than the S-shaped or Lebesgue curves in our scenario. In this scenario, the Hilbert and the Peano curves show superior locality properties. However, as the results of the Hilbert, Peano, and Fass2 curve though are close to each other, we analyze the behavior of the curves in another scenario.

	S-shaped	Lebesgue	Hilbert	Peano	Fass2
MER	0,33	0,33	0,26	0,26	0,27

Table 4.1: Mean Error Rate for each curve

4.4 Evaluation

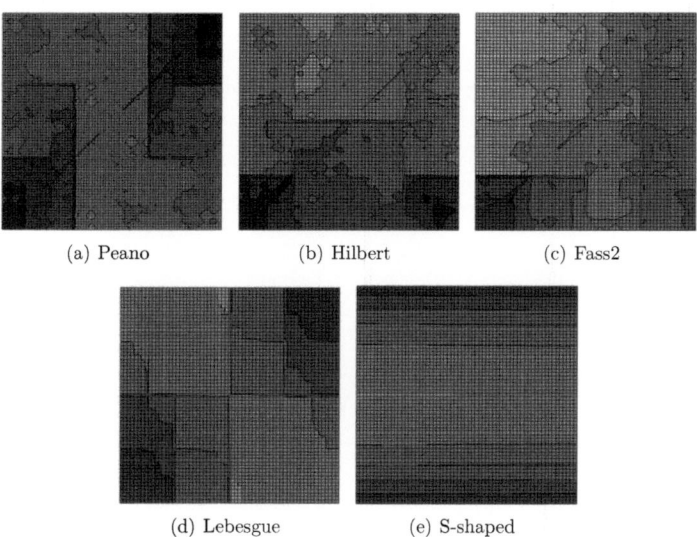

Figure 4.8: Mean Error Distribution of Space-Filling Curves

4.4.2 Small-World Populations

In this test we evaluated the curves using a more realistic scenario. Whereas in the latter test we calculated an average over all nodes, we now compare only a selection of nodes. This resembles the fact, that most likely not every zone will contain a node. There will be a some more interesting locations (Hotspots) and therefore, more nodes (Residents) will eventually be around. To reflect this natural behavior we used the Fermi-Dirac statistics [95] [96], assigning Hotspots and Residents to zones in the unit square, such that a small-world-like [97] population is mirrored. Small-world models have already been used to emulate real-life population scenarios [98]. Nodes (equivalent for people) within a certain proximity of each other form a cluster (e.g. a city). All clusters are randomly distributed and interconnected, thus resembling differently sized population areas. For our simulation, we first assigned one Resident randomly on the area. Further Residents will more likely populate a zone close to a zone, which is already populated, since this zone is more attractive. Afterwards, the Hotspots are placed in the near surroundings of larger Resident gatherings, since it is more likely that there is information to be stored than elsewhere. The curve in Figure 4.9(a) mirrors the level of attractiveness. The very near surrounding zones maintain a high level of attractiveness, which is dropping fast with an increasing distance. The unit square will thus contain some metropolitan areas and few scattered nodes, resembling heavy populated cities and less populated back-country. Thus, populations as in Figure 4.9(b) are generated.

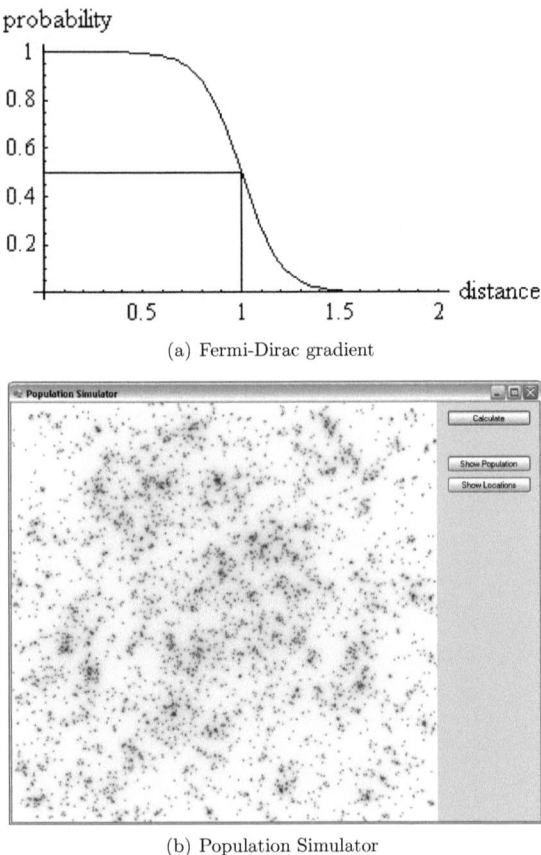

(a) Fermi-Dirac gradient

(b) Population Simulator

Figure 4.9: Generating small-world-like populations

The error rate in this case is calculated as follows. Each Hotspot i determines the node geographically closest $N_{Geo}(i)$ and the node closest in ID space $N_{ID}(i)$. Communication takes place with the node numerically closest to a Hotspot. An error occurs if the geographically closest node is not the node with the numerically closest ID. In this case, a more distant node will be contacted to deliver information

4.4 Evaluation

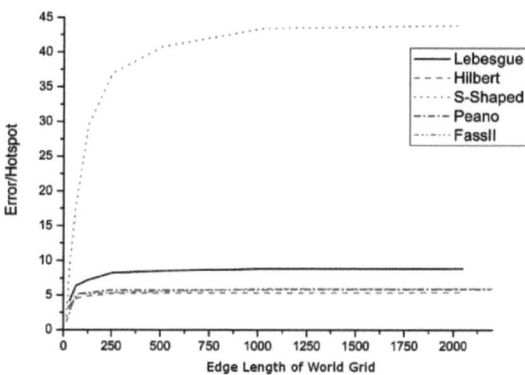

Figure 4.10: Linear Population Rate

about the Hotspot. Though we are talking about an error here, the system will nevertheless work. It is just the choice of nodes, which is sub-optimal. Thus, the small-world mean error rate (SMER) results from the euclidean difference between the optimal node N_{Geo} and the chosen node N_{ID}:

$$SMER_{curve} = \left\{ \sum_{i=1}^{n} \Delta geo\Big(N_{Geo}(i), N_{ID}(i)\Big) \Big| i \in Hotspots \right\} \quad (4.2)$$

In the first run we measure the error rate of the curves using a linear population rate as can be seen in Figure 4.10. The population p is dependent on the size of the grid (equivalent to the amount of zones the world is divided into), thus keeping the Hotspot/Resident ratio constant. It appears, that the SMER level of the more complex space-filling curves (Hilbert, Peano, Fass II) is far lower than that of the trivial curves. For this simulation we used a grid with up to 2048x2048 zones (see edge length in Figure 4.10). When partitioning the world for our peer-to-peer ring, the amount of zones will even be much higher. Therefore, the trivial curves pose no possible solution.

Another interesting aspect is to evaluate the performance of the different curves with varying population levels. Therefore, we kept the amount of Hotspots and Residents constant, regardless the size of the unit square and thus creating dense worlds at the beginning (with a smaller grid) to sparse networks (with a larger grid) as shown in Figure 4.11. It becomes obvious, that an efficient node-indexing cannot be achieved

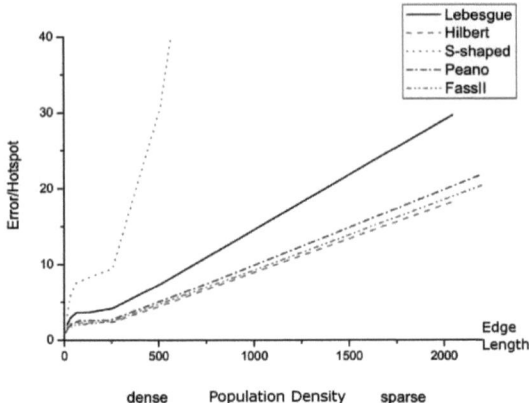

Figure 4.11: Error per Hotspot with dense and sparse populations

by using "simple" curves like the S-shaped or even the Lebesgue curve. This becomes clear when regarding worlds with a sparse population. The less Residents there are, the higher the probability to choose a geographically farther node over a closer one. The remaining curves perform almost equally, though the Hilbert curve shows the smallest error derivation.

4.5 Position Queries

Using the technical expertise from the preceding sections, we build the cornerstone for supporting spatial queries. To implement position queries, we have to take the geographic coordinates of the point of interest (POI) and calculate the appropriate index on the space-filling curve. The necessary calculations are presented in Algorithm 8, and a more detailed description of the used functions can be found in Tab. 4.2.

We receive the coordinates of the desired POI using GPS-receivers or similar devices. If the POI simply is the user's position, she or he can use a location-aware device (most mobile handsets already offer this technology) to retrieve the current coordinates. In most other cases freely available tools, such as Google Earth [28] or NASA's World Wind [99] do offer similar functionality. In the next step, we follow the suggestions of [100] and shift the origin 20° eastwards. Thus, we avoid South

4.5 Position Queries

Function	Description
GetCoordinates()	Retrieves coordinates.
Shift(POI)	Shift origin of the coordinate system 20° eastwards.
PeirceProjection(POI)	Apply Peirce Projection on POI.
Rotate(POI)	Rotate coordinate system by 45° around its center.
Translate(POI)	Translates projected coordinates onto new intervals.
HilbertIndex(POI)	Computes the POI's index on the Hilbert curve.

Table 4.2: Basic procedures used for implementing position queries

---

Algorithm 8 Pseudo code for calculating Hilbert Index for a POI

1: **function** CalcIndex(*POI*)
2: POI = GetCoordinates();
3: $POI_{Shifted}$ = Shift(*POI*);
4: $POI_{Projected}$ = PeirceProjection($POI_{Shifted}$);
5: $POI_{Rotated}$ = Rotate($POI_{Projected}$);
6: $POI_{Translated}$ = Translate($POI_{Rotated}$);
7: CurveIndex = HilbertIndex($POI_{Translated}$);
8: **return** CurveIndex;

America lying on a border line as this would lead to poor results for adjacent cities in South America. Eventually, the shifted POI gets projected using the above mentioned Peirce projection (see Appendix A). In the projection process the northern hemisphere is centered with the southern hemisphere split into 4 triangular parts which are aligned to the 4 borders of the northern hemisphere. The result has a diamond shape. For an easy mapping of the space-filling curve onto the projected map, we rotate the map by 45° in clockwise direction and thus receive a square-shaped map. The same procedure is valid for the projected POI (line 4). After the rotation, we translate the resulting point $p(x, y)$ from the preimage interval onto our "world" domain:

$$[-1.854 .. + 1.854] \stackrel{translate}{\rightarrow} [0 .. 2^{56}] \qquad (4.3)$$

For an easier understanding we omit the derivation of the preimage interval borders here and give a more detailed explanation in Appendix A. In the final step, we use the translated point ($POI_{Translated}$) as an input parameter for calculating the index on the Hilbert curve using the HilbertIndex function (see Alg. 12).

The calculated curve index then serves as a node ID and thus allows for position queries for any position on Earth. In the next step, we need to implement region and neighborhood queries. However, using the algorithm from above leads to an enormous computation effort as we would have to compute a huge amount of points to cover an entire region. This approach is therefore suitable for position queries only. In the following section we introduce another approach using a recursive approach. Thus, the computations take a little longer due to the recursion, but usually they do not have to run up to the highest resolution (the calculation process stops earlier). Furthermore, the recursion generates additional bits for the prefix of the node ID in each step. Thereby, we have a coarse result of nodes that actually lie in the requested region. This result is then refined in each recursion step until we exactly know which intervals of the curve index pass through the requested region.

4.6 Region Queries

Region queries entail a challenge compared to position queries. First, an area covers an indefinite amount points (here: positions). Thus, we need to find an efficient algorithm to determine all relevant node IDs for a specific region. Second, depending on the layout of the target region (shape and position on the world grid) it is possible, that the Hilbert curve dissects the region multiple times (see marked region in Fig. 4.12). This means, that the having the smallest and largest curve index for the target region does not suffice. We need to compute all intervals that pass the region. Therefore, we use a different approach making use of the regularity of the Hilbert SFC.

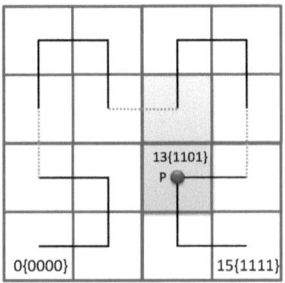

Figure 4.12: The requesting region intersects the curve twice

Through the analysis of the growth of the curve (see Fig. 4.6) we can derive the curve's building elements. The Hilbert curve consists of one major element with an

4.6 Region Queries

u-like shape being rotated and flipped such that we get the shapes $A - D$ as shown in Fig. 4.13.

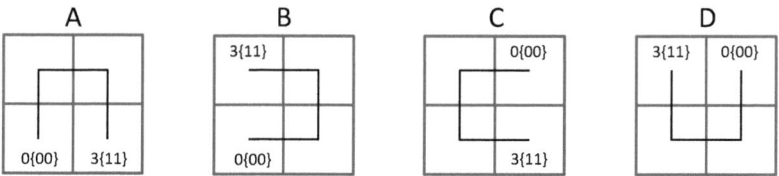

Figure 4.13: The elements of the Hilbert curve and the according prefixes

We set A's shape as origin of the order-1 Hilbert curve. So, to calculate the ID of the point P in Fig. 4.12 in the second-order Hilbert curve we have to calculate the ID in each step as we proceed. The generation of the ID depends on the state of the u and the choice of the next quadrant as shown in the following:

- The orientation in the first u-element is state A per definition. Point P lies in the lower right corner of the u and thus adds "11" to the ID.

- In the second step, we have to check the new orientation of the u-element and find it in state C. Point P now lies in the upper left corner. In combination with state C this adds a "01" to the prefix.

- In this example, our iteration ends here and we combine the prefixes of all steps to calculate the complete prefix for point $P_{ID} = 11_2 + 01_2 = 1101_2 = 13_{10}$.
  In general, we would have to repeat the second step until the "requested" region is completely covered by squares, generated through the iteration processes.

The procedure to generate the index for an arbitrary point respectively region can be expressed through a deterministic finite automaton (DFA) as shown in Fig. 4.14. We start in state A and depending on the input, switch to a new state (can also be state A again) and write some output: *input Σ/output Ω*. The resulting behavior can be simulated with a Mealy [101] machine, in which each state may act as a final state.

Definition 4.1 (Mealy Machine)
A Mealy machine is a 7-tuple, $(Q, \Sigma, \Omega, \delta, \lambda, q_0, F)$:

- Q is a finite set of states $(|Q| < \infty)$
- Σ is the input alphabet, $|\Sigma| < \infty, Q \cap \Sigma = \emptyset$
- Ω is the output alphabet, $|\Omega| < \infty$
- δ is the transition function: $\delta : Q \times \Sigma \to Q$
- λ defines the output: $\lambda : Q \times \Sigma \to \Omega$
- $q_0 \in Q$ is the starting state
- $F \subseteq Q$ is a finite amount of final states

For our purpose, we define the Mealy Machine as follows:

- $Q = \{A, B, C, D\}$, $\Sigma = \{0, 1, 2, 3\}$, $\Omega = \{00, 01, 10, 11\}$, $q_0 = \{A\}$, $F = \{A, B, C, D\}$
- δ and λ are defined through the flow as shown in Fig. 4.14

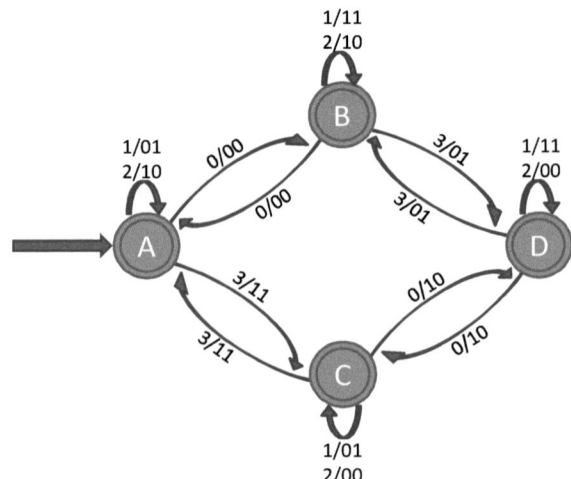

Figure 4.14: The DFA for generating the Hilbert Index (input Σ/ output Ω)

Region Queries: Index Calculation

As we now know how to calculate the ID for a specific region, supporting region queries is only a small step. We describe the essential algorithms in Alg. 9 respectively in Tab. 4.3.

The user enters the coordinates of the region for which she or he desires to find active peers. In the first step, the given region is passed onto the `FindSubRects` method, which divides the world (referring to the projected world layout as shown in Fig. 4.2) into four sub-squares. Consecutively, we check in which of the newly created sub-squares the requested region lies in. This leads to the following cases: First, the requested region is completely covered by one or more sub-squares the ID of the appropriate sub-squares (the generation of the ID follows the Mealy machine in Fig. 4.14). The IDs of the squares being a subset of the requested region are added to the *CurveIndexList*. Second, all sub-squares are larger than the requested region, then we continue the sub-dividing process and check the requested region again with the newly generated sub-square. Lastly, if there is no intersection between the requested region and the current sub-square, this computing branch is dropped. The algorithm stops when the requested region is completely covered by squares that have been generated through the above mentioned sub-division process.

Applying this algorithm onto the example presented in Fig. 4.12 (region query for the marked squares) we get a set of two IDs: $\{1000_2 = 8, 1101_2 = 13\}$. After the first partition, it becomes obvious that the first two sub-squares can be discarded as the marked region lies on the right hand side of the square. However, both of the sub-squares do not cover the region completely, but only partially. Therefore, the request is split and we continue to sub-divide the two sub-squares again into four sub-squares each. Checking all sub-squares again, we find sub-squares that do completely lie in the requested region, filling it entirely. Thus, their ID prefixes are also added to the *CurveIndexList*. As there are no more sub-squares that intersect with the requested region, the algorithm stops.

4.7 Neighborhood Queries

As we have shown how to implement region queries in the last section, neighborhood queries are just a small enhancement. Neighborhood queries determine all objects

Function	Description
`IntersectTest(Rect1, Rect2)`	Returns the overlap relation (*complete, partial, none*) between two rectangles.
`SubRects(X, Y, Height, Width)`	Takes the parent square and divides it into 4 sub-squares.
`FindSubRects(Rect, Region)`	"Divides the world" until *Region* is completely overlapped; then adds these rectangles.

Table 4.3: Basic procedures used for implementing region queries

---

Algorithm 9 Supporting Region Queries

1: **function** CalcIndices4RegionQuery(*ReqRegion*)
2:   `FindSubRects`(*Rect, ReqRegion*); // here *Rect* covers the whole world.
3:   **return** CurveIndexList;
4:
5: **function** FindSubRects(*Rect, ReqRegion*)
6:   `SubRects(Rect)`
7:   **for** $i = 0, i \leq 4, i++$ **do**
8:     **switch**(`IntersectTest`(*SubRect(i), ReqRegion*))
9:     **case** Complete:
10:       CurveIndexList.Add(*SubRect(i).ID*);
11:     **case** Partial:
12:       `FindSubRects`(*SubRect(i), ReqRegion*)
13:     **case** None:
14:       break;
15:     **end switch**
16:   **end for**

in a certain perimeter around one's position, e.g. "which restaurants are closer than 1.500 meters to my current position?" as shown in Fig. 4.15.

Thus, the desired region has a circular shape with a diameter of 1.500 meters and its center at the user's location. So, we reduce the neighborhood query to a region query of the same region. Depending on the desired accuracy of the results, we can divide the circular shape into n rectangles. The higher the amount of rectangles, the better we can converge the region query to the actual neighborhood query.

Thus, it's up to the user to decide the trade-off between too little and too many results. In our example, using a low accuracy might lead to the drop-out of restaurant A.

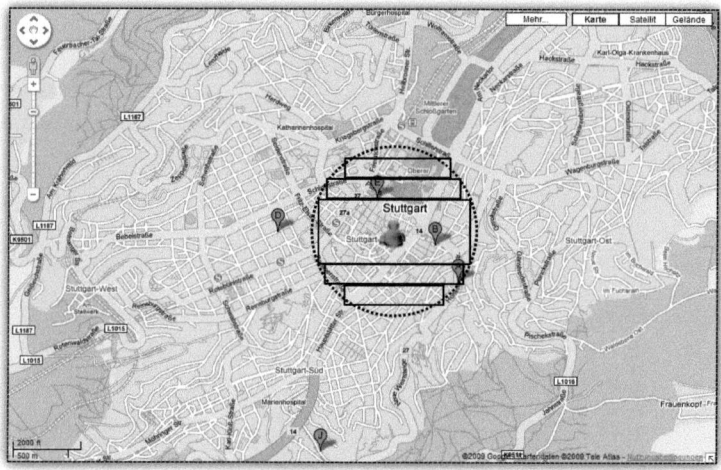

Figure 4.15: Approximating a neighborhood query through multiple region queries

4.8 Summary

In this chapter, we have presented a method allowing to host location-based information in a self-organizing peer-to-peer system. In contrast to existing context-based systems our algorithm optimizes the data distribution towards geometrical locality, keeping the distance information travels short. We showed that finding an optimal curve for node-indexing is not a simple problem, as the S-shaped and even the more complex Lebesgue curve perform poorly. The more complex SFC present far better locality properties, especially the Hilbert curve. As Hilbert's average derivation error in small-world-like world partitions is also very low, the curve is perfectly suited for the use in our scenario.

Through the Peirce map projection we are able to represent Earth as a 2-dimensional square. On this map, the user may choose a point or an area for her or his query. By fitting the Hilbert curve on top of the map we can calculate the index for the appropriate node IDs. For a single POI, the user enters geographical coordinates and gets a single ID. The peer then sends its query towards this ID. Though it is very likely that the peer with this exact ID does not exist, the query will reach a node close to the desired location by applying Pastry's prefix routing.

We have presented two approaches on how to use the Hilbert curve for calculating the appropriate node IDs. The first approach calculates the curve index through projections, transformations, and further mathematical computations. Thus, it runs rather fast, however lacks an efficient solution to region or neighborhood queries. The second approach is rather computational intense, however allows for a faster calculation of the curve indices for a specific region.

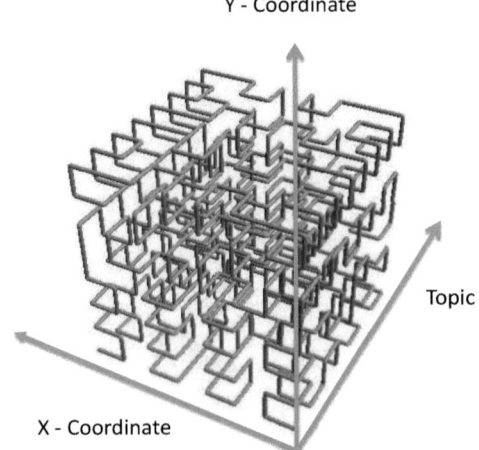

Figure 4.16: The Hilbert curve in 3D based on [102]

When sending a region or a neighborhood query, the result will contain a set of IDs. In this case, the querying peer uses a suitable protocol (e.g. multicast) to send the

4.8 Summary

query to the active peers in the desired region. Thereby, we allow for the major types of spatial queries and thus fulfill the requirements for a location-based system using peer-to-peer technology.

At this moment, our system only supports location-based searches. However, it is unlikely that all participating peers in the overlay provide information of the same topic. Therefore, we propose the extension of our system by introducing another classification option. We enhance our x & y coordinate system by a z-axis denoting the covered topic. The topics are organized using a pre-defined taxonomy. Thus, we can hash a certain topic and receive a value for the z-axis. The node ID can then be calculated anew to reflect a location and a major topic. The Hilbert curve thus needs to cover 3 dimensions, forming an information cube as shown in Fig. 4.16. Through slicing and dicing operations similar to those in on-line analytical processing (OLAP) new query types are possible. The user can now search either for a certain topic or all topics on a certain location or a combination of both. As a peer may provide information covering more than one topic, it may become necessary for a single peer to use multiple node IDs. The overhead for using multiple node IDs in terms of routing etc. however has yet to be determined.

Chapter 5

Replication

In this chapter, we present a replication algorithm for peer-to-peer networks that automatically adapts to an increase of requests. If some information suddenly becomes very popular, the algorithm distributes it in the peer-to-peer system and reduces the replicas when the demand decreases. The algorithm is totally self-organizing, i.e. it does not need any administration and is very resilient to node failures. Furthermore, our algorithm uses the concept of geographical proximity. Data is preferably replicated on peers which are geographically close. This is especially useful for location-based information, such as traffic information, tourist data and weather alerts.

5.1 Introduction

Peer-to-peer systems (P2P) are known to scale well with respect to the amount of data offered by the system, thus they work perfectly for large video files or software downloads. However, current systems fail to adapt to "hot topics", i.e. if a certain information suddenly attracts many users, the system should replicate the data on an increasing number of peers [103]. Once the interest in the topic has passed the peak, the number of replicas can be reduced again.

This is a serious issue: an open-source project offering high-resolution pictures on its website "suffers" from a post on a major blog (e.g. engadget.com or slashdot.org). The same may happen to a news website offering videos about special events (e.g. an important soccer game). Both services are rendered unavailable in a matter of hours, as the amount of request shortly surpasses the capabilities of the respective service providers. However, a few days later this information will hardly be requested any more.

The P2P replication mechanism we are presenting in this chapter automatically detects and replicates often requested information. Furthermore, our system is very resilient towards peer failures, because there is no central point of failure. In contrast, systems such as Bittorrent [1] can easily be taken down by stopping the so-called tracker. Our system is totally self-organizing. Thus, a highly requested topic cannot become unavailable because a small set of peers goes offline.

Our approach takes the locality of information in consideration, allowing us to store and retrieve information for geographical regions. The replication mechanism presented in this chapter always tries to replicate data on peers, which are geographically close to the origin of the data. In the example of a traffic jam, this information will preferably be stored on peers near the traffic jam. One reason for this is to reduce overall network load. For example, there is no reason to host traffic information about Cologne on a peer in Madrid. Another reason is to avoid free riders [78], i.e. peers who download but do not intend to upload data. If a peer computer hosts data that is relevant to the owner of the computer, the owner has an incentive to offer some of his network capacities for the topic.

Replication in peer-to-peer systems is fundamentally different from replication in server-based environments. Servers are costly and therefore they should be used to full capacity most of the time. In contrast, a peer-to-peer system consists of thousands of personal or mobile computers which are most of the time idle. Thus, it is relatively easy to find an idle peer. The major challenge in our scenario is the self-organization, i.e. automatically detecting and replicating hot topics and dealing with peers that suddenly leave the network.

In the sections below, we detail the goals and challenges of our algorithm, followed by a brief repeat of Geostry's locality properties in Section 5.3. Subsequently, we present our algorithm and evaluate it in Section 5.5 to show how it adapts to various scenarios and close with a short summary.

5.2 Replication Goals & Challenges

In this section, we describe the requirements that should be met by a replication technique which is P2P-based and location-aware. Thereby, we illustrate the challenges that arise when using replication in peer-to-peer systems. General requirements for peer-to-peer systems [10] (e.g. scalability, efficiency...) are covered by the peer-to-peer system itself and therefore not regarded in this work.

1. **Durability**: The main objective of durability is that information should not get lost. To strengthen this goal, data can be replicated to redundant locations.

2. **Availability**: Objects need to be accessible at all times. This includes the durability of data. However, data can be durable without being available. This is the case whenever the provider of a datum is "overloaded" and cannot reply to incoming queries. To provide a high level of availability, replicas need to be distributed over the network, thereby also minimizing the effect of potential network failures.

3. **Flash-Crowd-Proof**: When a specific information abruptly receives a burst in popularity, the host often becomes unavailable due to the sudden increase in traffic. These boosts are unpredictable and may occur at any time. Servers then suffer from the so-called *slashdot-effect* [103, 104]. To cope with this effect, counter-measures have to be initiated in time.

4. **Fast Discovery**: Having many replicas does not necessarily improve the overall system performance. It is crucial to discover replicas efficiently.

5. **Economic**: A fast discovery can be easily implemented with a high number of replicas. However, an intelligent and economic replication scheme should only generate as much replicas as needed to satisfy all incoming request.

6. **Commitment**: Peers implicitly have to accept to host information from foreign peers. Without this commitment any peer-to-peer network suffers from the freerider problem. On one hand we rely on the enthusiasm of the users to participate in our system while on the other hand we optimized our system such that users rather store information about their immediate vicinity than from the opposite side of the world. Furthermore, we refer to [78] offering various methods to counter the freerider problem.

5.3 System Model

In Chapter 4 we presented Geostry with its location properties suited for a location-based information system on a peer-to-peer basis. Geostry is based on Pastry [37] and thus belongs to the latest generation of P2P systems. For addressing a value distributed hash table (DHT) systems mostly use a 128-bit identifier. In Pastry, these IDs are generated by applying a hash function to the IP address, which guarantees unique IDs. Given a message and a key, Pastry routes a message to the node with the node ID numerically closest to the key. In each routing step the message reaches a node sharing an ID-prefix (with the destination object) at least one digit longer, therefore reaching the target in $\lceil \log_{2^b} n \rceil$ steps (assuming an accurate routing table, also see Section 2.2.2). As Pastry hashes over the IP address, a numerically small hop may actually lead to a huge jump in terms of geographic distance.

In contrast to Pastry, with Geostry we achieve locality of data. Peers which are geographically close to each other in the real world should therefore exhibit numerically close IDs in the node ID space. Therefore, we link the node IDs to the physical location of the node in a special way. In the last chapter we have shown how to use space-filling curves to achieve that goal. Furthermore, nodes in Pastry, as well as in Geostry, use a leafset to keep track of nodes with similar node IDs. As Geostry implements locality, the leafset nodes (*leafs*) are also in the near vicinity of the node. In the next section we will illustrate the use of these nodes for replication purposes.

Additionally, the combination of locality and distributed hash tables leads to fast converging routes. That is, the distance per hop decreases in the direction of the target node, quickly putting the query geographically close the original provider of the data. This feature as well may be used for a fast information retrieval, as can be seen in Section 5.4.5. In Geostry, the majority of peers runs on a rather low load. This derives from the fact, that at one point in time only a few peers offer highly interesting information. The main goal of the replication mechanisms in Geostry therefore lies in dampening the peaks when many peers request data from a single peer. In contrast to peer-to-peer systems administrators of larger data centers (e.g. Amazon) usually expect their servers to run on high loads (Google [105] talks about 70-80%). Due to these different assumptions, we cannot adopt the replication mechanisms used in data centers.

Function	Description
UsedBandwith(req_{in})	Returns the bandwidth used for handling all incoming requests.
SendReplica(*peer*)	Sends a snapshot to a given *peer*.
HashKey(*it, data*)	Returns the it^{th} hash value to a given data element.
FreeReplica(*id, peer*)	Allows a *peer* to delete a replica with a specific *identifier*.
SendLowUsage(*peer*)	Informs a given *peer* about a decreased request rate.
SendLeaveAck(*bool, peer*)	Allows/Denies a *peer* to leave the replica group
SendRemoteDeny(*peer*)	Informs the *creator* that the load is too high to become its *remote*.
SendRemoteAck(*peer*)	Informs the *creator* that it accepts becoming its *remote*.

Table 5.1: Basic procedures during replication

5.4 Replication Design

In Geostry as in other distributed hash table based P2P systems, nodes use a hash function to calculate which peer is responsible for hosting the desired information. More precisely, a peer applies the hash function on a topic or a keyword (this might also be a location), which leads to a *key*. In the next step, the peer generates a query with this key as a target address. For an easier understanding we depict all peers inserting information of their own to the overlay network as *creator*. The peer with the node ID the closest to that target address - this *creator* - is responsible for the sought-after topic respectively keyword. Depending on the state of the peer the query is sent to, different actions need to be taken.

5.4.1 State 1: Direct object access

In our peer-to-peer system, we subdivide the replication process into three states (see Figure 5.1(a)). At the beginning, the *creator* is able to satisfy all incoming requests req_{in} on its own. Therefore, no replication is needed in State 1.

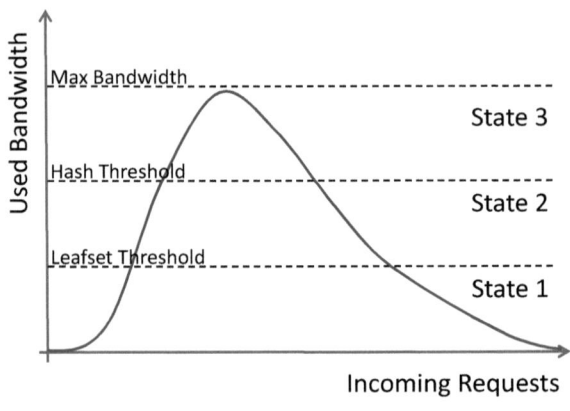

(a) Replications States

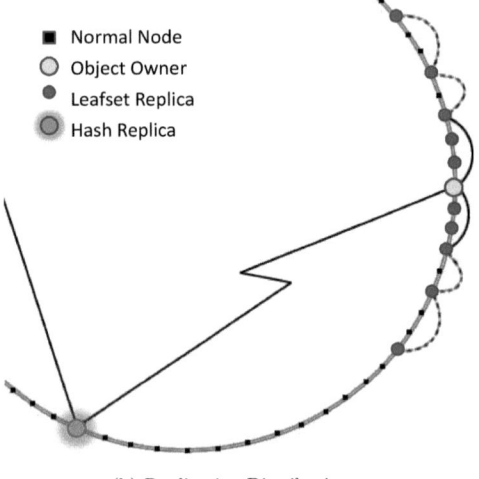

(b) Replication Distribution

Figure 5.1: Illustration of Geostry's replication behavior

5.4.2 State 2: Leafset Redirection

With an increasing interest in the information provided by a specific host, the load increases as well. If no special action is taken, the load will increase until the point where the bandwidth per request is getting lower and lower while new requests cannot be answered at all. Therefore, as soon as the amount of incoming requests reaches the *LeafsetThreshold*, the data is replicated on the leafset nodes indicating State 2 (see Algorithm 10). Further incoming requests are not answered anymore, but redirected to a node from leafset. The peer may do so as it is aware of its current load situation: e.g. in asynchronous Digital Subscriber Line (DSL) networks the download capabilities usually are a lot higher than the upload ones. In symmetric networks both channels have equal bandwidth, but the query is still smaller in size than the response. Thus, the peer is able to notice when the upload capabilities are depleted though further queries keep arriving.

For fairness reasons we use the round robin method when choosing the redirection peer. In doing so, the *creator* distributes the load to peers in the near geographical surrounding. Wolfson's [106] showed that requests for geographical-related information mostly originate from the immediate vicinity. By distributing replicas to *leafs* - which in Geostry are the closest peers nearby - we take advantage of this theorem. At this state, the *creator* may leave the network as one of his *leafs* will take its place.

Algorithm 10 Check whether to start Leafset Replication
1: **procedure** CheckLeafsetReplication()
2: **if** (UsedBandwidth() > *LeafsetThreshold*)
    & (UsedBandwidth() < *HashThreshold*) **then**
3:    **for all** (*Peer* in *Leafset*) **do**
4:       SendReplica(*Peer*);
5:    **end for**
6: **end if**

5.4.3 State 3: Timeout - Deterministic Alternatives

In the third state, the amount of incoming requests surpasses the limit of requests that a peer can answer and redirect. Thus, some requesting peers will encounter a timeout while waiting for the *creator* to answer. As the requesting peers cannot guess the *creator*'s leafset, they need a well-known algorithm to find another peer

with a replica. To do so, the requesting peer applies the hash function:
HashKey(1, topic)=ID1 → HashKey(2, topic)=ID2 and so on. Each hash operation results in a new key. This peer which is responsible for the new key located far away, we call *remote*. This *remote* itself will start in State 1 and answer incoming queries. In case the load at the *remote* surpasses the *LeafsetThreshold* it will shift to State 2 and start redirecting to its own leafset.

The amount of replicas (*NrOfRemotes*) that are generated at remote peers can be configured dynamically at the creator (see Algorithm 11), eliminating the need for *remotes* to switch to State 3. To guarantee a fair load distribution, we apply the SHA-1 [34] algorithm for the hash operations. Figure 5.1(b) illustrates how replicas are distributed on the P2P ring. For this book, we assume all nodes have homogeneous capabilities. However, we can easily increase *NrOfRemotes* to minimize the probability of choosing a "weak" (in terms of computing power, bandwidth, etc.) node as *remote*.

In the unlikely event, that a chosen *remote* is already running on high load, it may send a SendRemoteDeny(*creator*) instead of a SendRemoteAck(*creator*) message. In doing so, the *creator* simply applies the Hashkey(*x+1, topic*) again to find the next suitable peer to take the role of a *remote*. However, as we assume that the majority of peers runs on low loads, this case is rather uncommon.

Algorithm 11 Check whether to start Hash Replication

1: **procedure** CheckHashReplication()
2:   **if** UsedBandwidth() > *HashThreshold* **then**
3:     *targetRemotes* := 0;
4:     $x := 0$;
5:     **while** (*targetRemotes* < *NrOfRemotes*) **do**
6:       *remote[x]* := HashKey(x, *data element*);
7:       SendReplica(*remote[x]*);
8:       **if received** SendRemoteAck **then**
9:         *targetRemotes*++;
10:       **end if**
11:       x++;
12:     **end while**
13:   **end if**

5.4.4 Replication Clean-Up

As the disk space on all participating peers is finite, we have to limit the degree of replication over time. Without any further limitations, replicas would remain on a multitude of peers though the demand for this specific information has decreased or even ceased completely. On the other hand we want to guarantee durability. Therefore, we have to find a trade-off between the amount of replicas and the time the replicas are being hold at the foreign peers.

The *creator* solely decides on the amount of *remotes*, depending on the estimated required bandwidth. After this, the *remotes* act autonomously and decide on how many *leafs* they themselves send the replica to. In doing so, the *remotes* fairly distribute the load to their neighbors. Considering the overall load for a specific data element it is the highest at the *creator*, followed by its *leafs* and then the *remotes* with their *leafs*. This makes it easy to adapt the amount of replicas to the actual need in the network.

As the *remotes* decide locally when to forward replicas to their *leafs*, they can also delete these replicas. In case the amount of arriving queries at the *remote* drops under a certain threshold (the *FreeLeafThreshold*), it sends a `FreeReplica(id, leafs)` message to some or all of its *leafs*. This allows them to destroy their replicas and free their memory. Later on, when the amount of queries has dropped under the *FreeRemoteThreshold*, the *remote* informs the *creator* about this circumstance (`SendLowUsage(creator)`) and waits for a reply. If the load at the *creator* is low enough such that the *creator* can handle the *remote*'s incoming requests itself, it accepts the *remote*'s request for leaving the replica group (`SendLeaveAck(true, remote)`). Then, the *remote* frees its memory and makes it available for other replicas. If the load at the *creator* is still too high, it denies the request and the *remote* stays in the replica group.

If the *creator* leaves the network, while it still has replicas on other peers, incoming queries may still be answered. If requests for the *creator*'s data keep coming, the *leafs* and/or *remotes* will still respond to them. However, as the request rate drops, their soft-state mechanism will lead to the deletion of the *creator*'s data. Therefore, the *creator* has no guarantee, that its data will still be available once the *creator* itself left the network. This is done intentionally, we do not want another *leaf* to take over the role of the *creator* forever. As we assume that the creator initially introduced the data to the overlay network, we presume that it is safe to remove the data as soon as the creator does not offer the data itself any more and it is no longer requested (we keep a safety time in case the creator suffers from a short error (e.g. network failure, reboot, etc.). In our scenario, we envision users to provide dynamic information (e.g. sensor information), which is usually getting outdated after a short period of time. Putting this data on other peers, which are providing data themselves would pose a high load on other peers. Therefore, we only provide durability (see requirements in Section 5.2) as long as the original contributor stays in the network. Additionally, this action helps fighting freeriders as it is no use joining the network, generating replicas and leave the network afterwards: its data will eventually time out and not remain in the overlay.

5.4.5 Fast Converging Routes

As we mentioned before, Geostry features fast converging routes [107]. This feature results from the prefix-routing and the locality of data. The first hops will differ greatly in the first few bits, resulting in a large geographical distance being traveled between these hops. As the key of the peers the query is passing gets closer to the key of the target node, the geographical distance between the hops gets lower.

For our replication purposes we can take advantage of this characteristic. After the *creator* of a well-queried information changed to State 2, information is replicated to other nodes of his leafset. These *leafs* are chosen as they are listed in the *creator's* leafset and thus are in its near geographical surrounding. This in turn means, that the ID of those nodes does not differ a lot from the *creator*. In doing so, we replicate information around the location it is about. This allows the *creator* to leave the network (at least for a short time) without rendering its information unaccessible. Furthermore, there is the effect of the fast converging routes. As the amount of queries for this specific information increases, queries eventually pass by nodes, which already store a replica. This is due to the routing protocol in Pastry. Peers, who do not know the *creator* (respectively have an entry in their routing table) forward the query to a peer with a node ID which is closer than their own. Thus, the query possibly hits a *leaf* and does not need to be forwarded any more, but can be answered locally. Thereby, in addition to the replication itself, the load on the *creator* can be further reduced as it does not has to perform any redirection in this case.

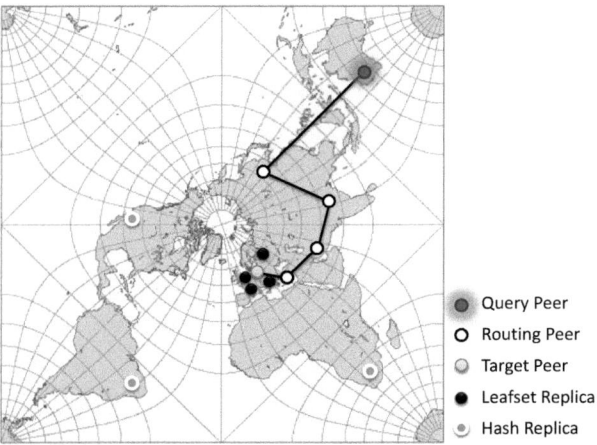

Figure 5.2: Fast Converging Routes

5.5 Evaluation

To document the adaptability under varying load situations we implemented a simulator in C#. We consecutively generate 1000 nodes and integrate them into the overlay using Pastry's *Join* method. Thereby, the routing tables of each peer are getting filled and each peer keeps an average of 6 connections to other peers. Incoming requests are answered directly by the responsible peer (called the *creator*) if possible. If more requests arrive, they are redirected to the *leafs* until the peer processes up to 30 requests in parallel. From this point on, queries remain unanswered and their senders thus have to use the HashKey(*topic*) method to find a suitable *remote*. In our evaluation peers need between 30 and 180 ms to process a query, resulting in an average throughput of 9.5 requests/second. When a peer acts as *leafs* or *remotes* we reduce its throughput up to a tenth of the *creator's*. Thus, the peer is still able to host its own data without being affected by "supporting" other peers too much. For the evaluation below we assign eight *leafs* to each peer and calculate four *remotes*. To fortify our simulations, we implement a packet drop mechanism into the network. This mechanism skips queries randomly between 0 and 10 percent, imitating connection problems and temporary failures.

5.5.1 Scenarios

Our evaluation is based on the three most typical usage patterns.

Constant: By simulating a constant rate of interest for a specific piece of information, we can simulate the general behavior for information of average interest. This illustrates the routing behavior, which applies to the majority of data. Therefore, we have the request rate for a specific piece of information in this scenario cycling between 12 and 14 requests per second.

Wave: If information about a certain event (e.g. information about traffic conditions shortly before rush hour) increasingly becomes more and more important, the overall request rate for this information will rise steadily. However, after some time, the information will get obsolete (most people are at home) and the request rate will drop again. In this scenario, we model this wave-like behavior in regular recurrences by using a request rate cycling between 10 and a 100 requests/second.

Surge: In case a certain piece of information becomes important for a large group of peers (e.g. an earthquake happened and lots of users want to check for available information about it), the request rate will erratically rise far above the capabilities a peer can handle. Therefore, all states of the replication process will be used. To simulate this behavior, we set the request rate to 8.3 requests per second at the beginning, which is then rapidly rising to a maximum of 50 requests/second.

5.5.2 Results and Analysis

One of the major challenges we address in this chapter is the ability to adapt the replication to various different scenarios. We had six runs per scenario all showing the same behavior. A measurement as depicted in Fig. 5.3 illustrates how often a request was handled by each "role".

We have classified these scenarios into three categories according to their stress level. As we can see in Fig. 5.4(a), a constant low level of queries leads to the fact that the *creator* is able to handle most of the queries on its own. After eight seconds, the time to answer a query takes longer (simulating more complex queries) and thus a few more peers (*leafs* and *remotes*) are needed to compensate the amount of queries. Fig. 5.3(a) shows that over time, the *creator* is able to handle around 90% of queries on its own. In the wave scenario (see Fig. 5.4(b)), we see that the

5.5 Evaluation

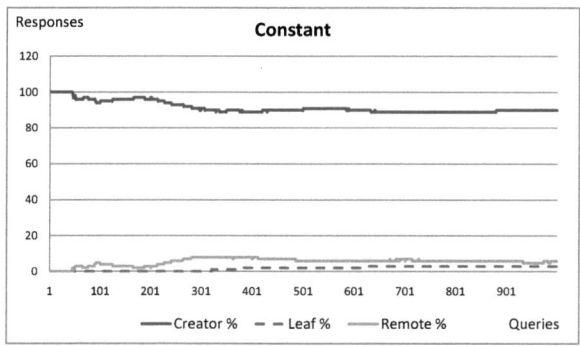

(a) Accumulated Constant

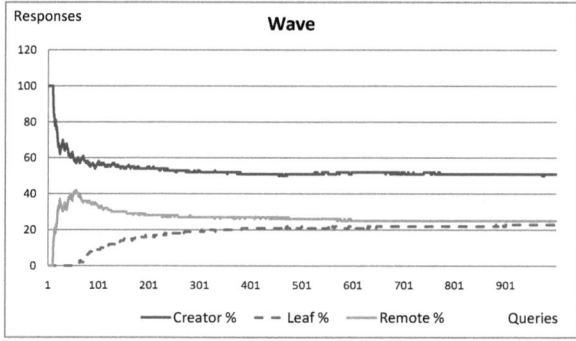

(b) Accumulated Wave

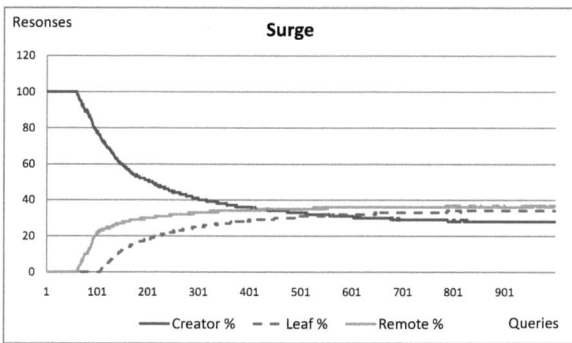

(c) Accumulated Surge

Figure 5.3: Replication simulation (accumulated) using 1000 peers

creator handles all queries until the interest in a topic gets too high. Then, the *leafs* and the *remotes* take part in the replication process and answer queries, too. As the interest decreases, the replica clean-up phase starts and removes replicas from *leafs and remotes*. Thus, the *creator* solely answers all queries, not needing further peers any more. On average, the *creator* answers around 50% itself (see Fig. 5.3(b)), leaving the remainder for the *leafs* and *remotes*. The surge scenario (see Fig. 5.4(c)) shows what happens in times of high loads. All participating peers run at their limit to answer the incoming queries. In general (see Fig. 5.3(c)), the *creator* answers even less queries than the peers hosting the replicas. This is due to a shift in the *creator*'s task, since it does much more redirecting than answering queries directly.

The kind of peer answering a query changes in relation to the current load. In times of low loads, the *creator* handles all traffic, whereas in times of high interest in its data, the *leafs* and *remotes* add to the *creator*'s bandwidth and answer a major part of the queries. This shows, that our replication scheme is able to adapt to the required bandwidth and processing load.

5.6 Summary

Solving the replication problem within peer-to-peer systems is a challenging task. The adaptation to flash-crowds requires a dynamic replication scheme, which also provides robustness in terms of node churn. In this chapter, we presented a solution - solely based on local decision making - to overcome this challenge. Thereby, we combine existing concepts from PAST [40] (*leafset replication*, see Section 6.4.5) and enhance them by an efficient replica distribution and a dynamic replication factor.

In the event of a high interest in a certain topic, data is replicated to nearby nodes at first. If the arising load exceeds the bandwidth, being offered by the *creator* and its leaf nodes, a hash function is used to determine other peers, which will store further replicas. In this case, a peer searching for information about this "hot topic" will possibly receive a timeout when searching for the information at the *creator*. Therefore, it applies a well-known hash function to find other peers, which also provide this information. The amount of replicas self-adapts to the demand, in terms of replicas being generated in times of great demand and deleted when the demand falls. Thus, we can eliminate the effect of peaks and satisfy the replication

5.6 Summary

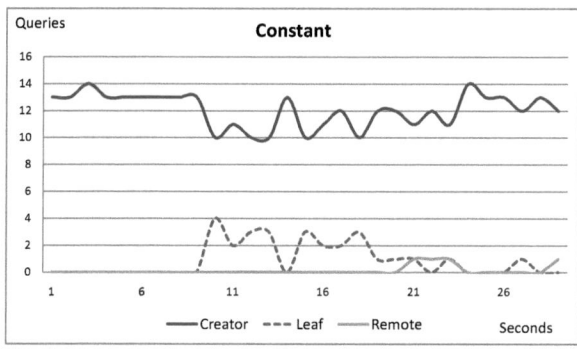

(a) Load Distribution: Constant

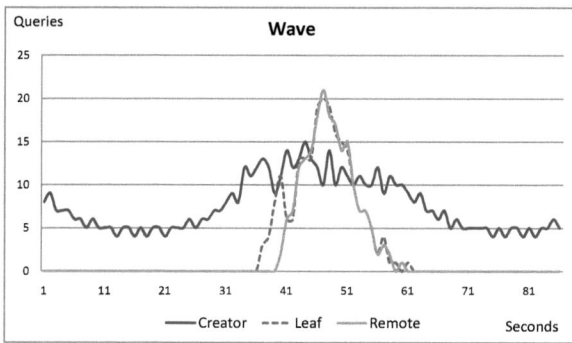

(b) Load Distribution: Wave

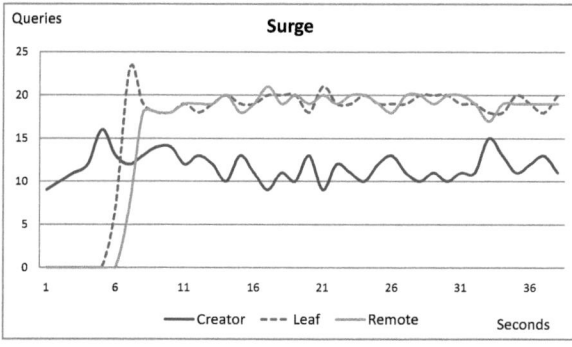

(c) Load Distribution: Surge

Figure 5.4: Replication simulation using 1000 peers showing the Load Distribution

goals (see Section 5.2). Though our algorithms are optimized for a location-based peer-to-peer system, they can be adapted to fit standard DHT-based systems.

Chapter 6

Related Work

In this chapter, we give a detailed overview of all the subjects we touched in this work. We thereby list the major publications and projects dealing with similar scenarios and differentiate Geostry from them. For the main contributions of this work, we have added a section with the corresponding related work.

6.1 P2P-based location service

To our knowledge there is no other framework for hosting context-data, which is based on P2P technology and optimizes for locality of their content. However, there has been excessive research in partial aspects of our project. In this section we present some of Geostry's tasks that have not been covered by a dedicated chapter. These tasks cover P2P systems in general, data storage and distribution. To illustrate the uniqueness of our scenario, we highlight the most popular representative for each task and briefly analyze them to show that they are not suited for our purpose.

6.1.1 P2P Systems: CAN

Protocols in this section are optimized towards the main tasks of P2P systems: insertion, lookup, and deletion of keys. CAN [108] is a popular and efficient representative of this section. Its storage mechanisms are similar to Pastry's, but its routing algorithm differs. CAN's coordinate space is completely logical and bears no relation to any physical coordinate system [109]. Hence it is difficult to host context-information according to its location as peers are responsible for a randomly chosen zone. Even if we assign the zones according to the node's position, in the defragmentation process nodes are eventually assigned a completely different zone, thus losing all geographical relation. Furthermore, the coordinate space is partitioned dynamically which requires many updates of neighborhood nodes in the case of new nodes or node failure. Thus, its runtime of $O(\frac{d \cdot N^{1/d}}{4})$ is worse than Pastry's $O(log(N))$. However, CAN optimizes for routing, whereas we want to optimize for locality of data.

6.1.2 Data Storage: OceanStore

This area deals with storage problems and how to spread large amounts of data among all peers most adequately. One of the largest projects in that area is the OceanStore [19], [110] project. Its main research focuses on a utility infrastructure for providing continuous access to persistent information. OceanStore distinguishes between service providers and users who subscribe to one of these providers. The providers are comprised of untrusted servers, which raises the necessity to replicate all data on several other servers to prevent a loss. Therefore, OceanStore is less suited for hosting context-based information.

6.1.3 Data Distribution

Data distribution covers the aspects of sharing information with an arbitrary amount of users. Whereas doing so with a small amount of users is a quite simple task, this does not apply for larger numbers due to bandwidth problems. Therefore, more intelligent strategies have to be utilized.

Bittorrent

Another technique that has become popular for spreading media data (e.g. movies) or large software packets (e.g. linux distributions, OpenOffice, etc.) is Bittorrent [111], [1]. Files are simply split into thousands of chunks and then distributed in a tit-for-tat-like manner to prevent freeriding. That is peers have to upload chunks again or the download will cease. Each peer tries to maximize its download rate by primarily contacting peers with high bandwidth. After successfully downloading the file, the peer may become a seed, continue to stay online, and allow free downloads. To download a file, the user has to get the corresponding *.torrent* file, which points to a tracker, that maintains a global registry of all downloaders and seeds. The tracker responds to a download query with a list of peers having (at least parts of) the file. The popularity (over 50% of all P2P traffice in 2004) confirms its efficiency, however the .torrent files are only found using web sites which act as global directories of available files. This makes it difficult to provide sensor data as dynamic data would result in new files which would have to be distributed anew. Therefore, the use of Bittorrent in the area of location-based services is highly unlikely.

Avalanche

This research area deals with the distribution of large files to a large user base. For companies like Microsoft this is an essential problem as they have to provide users of their software with the appropriate security fixes and product updates. With Avalanche [112] Microsoft Research developed a tool using network coding algorithms to solve this problem. The main technical innovation bases on the introduction of network coding techniques into the distribution process. This mechanism is not new, however has never been used in this context before. In principle, each node is capable of generating and transmitting encoded blocks of information. Randomization was introduced into the encoding process to improve the scheduling of block propagation and make the distribution more efficient. More precisely, instead of distributing the blocks of the files, those participating peers produce linear combinations of the blocks they already have. These combinations are then tagged with a description of the parameters used for the encoding and then distributed. Any peer receiving these combinations can generate new unique combinations from the ones it has downloaded so far. When the peer has received enough independent combinations, it can decode and build the original file. Avalanche is optimized in a similar fashion as OceanStore for it is designed to distribute persistent data to a larger user group. Sensor-data however is very small and often only interesting for few users. This makes the protocol inappropriate for the distribution of context-data.

6.2 Bootstrapping

There are several different approaches on how to discover a peer in an overlay network. In the following, we distinguish between two classes, namely the peer-based approaches and the mediator-based approaches.

6.2.1 Peer-based approaches

Nodes applying the peer-based approach are trying to directly detect and contact peers of the overlay network. After exchanging communication with regular peers, they gain information for joining the network themselves. Some approaches that imply this procedure are peer caches, random probing and various *cast protocols.

Peer Cache

Using *peer caches* is one of the simplest approaches, yet it proves to be effective. After signing off from the overlay network, a peer stores the addresses of all other peers that it has been connected to in its cache, which is then written to stable storage. On the next attempt to join the overlay, the peer loads its cache and tries to connect to the enlisted nodes directly. If one or more peers answer, the node may use them to join the network. This approach is therefore simple, efficient, robust and scalable. However, in the case that none of the peers from the peer cache is active and currently present in the overlay, the bootstrapping process will fail.

Random Probing

It is also possible to use *random probing* in order to bootstrap a node. To do so, a node tries to randomly connect to another node in the communication network by sending messages over a distinct port [42]. In case the contacted node is a peer, it replies, otherwise the node generates a new IP address and tries to contact this one. Random probing therefore works well in dense networks with a high peer to node ration, however, it is not suited for starting a new overlay network and bootstrapping the first nodes. In the latter case, nodes might have to generate a huge amount of connections until a participating peer of the overlay is found. Furthermore, the robustness against security appliances is not given, as firewalls or

6.2 Bootstrapping

NAT routers may prevent opening a connection on novel ports. This method could be further improved if security appliances are enhanced with heuristics to distinguish between a bootstrapping process and a virus or worm attack.

Broadcast

Similar in simplicity is Foner's Yenta approach [113] in which *broadcasts* are used for bootstrapping. A node sends out a UDP broadcast, querying for peers of the overlay. As gateway routers do not forward broadcast messages, the node will only get a reply if there is an active peer in the local area network. Thus, this approach only works in very dense networks or in combination with other bootstrapping approaches. However, peers in highly populated networks listening to those bootstrap broadcasts need to implement a random delay in their responses or messages will be dropped due to collisions resulting from packet storms.

Multicast

Cramer et al. propose another reliable and convenient bootstrapping method in [42]. All peers out of the same local area network join a common group using the *multicast* protocol. When a node wants to join the overlay network, it sends a query to the multicast group and receives the IP addresses of the other participants in return. This allows for a simple and efficient bootstrapping process. A crucial factor for the success of this method is the support of the multicast protocol across several network domains. As for now, it cannot be used in a world-spanning communication network as multicast packets are discarded at most routers.

Anycast

For a successful bootstrap, it is sufficient to contact one peer out of the overlay. This is the very idea of *anycast*. The new node sends a message to the P2P group, not addressing a specific peer. The recipient of the message is determined through the routing, more specific, the topologically closest node to the sender will receive the message and answers with information about further nodes. To realize bootstrapping with anycast, each P2P network needs its own anycast address. However, this is one of the reasons why the anycast approach will not scale nowadays [43] [114] as it is incredibly wasteful with IP addresses. The routing infrastructure only accepts IP prefixes with 24 bits, therefore a single anycast address consumes 256 IP addresses. Larger prefixes would lead to huge routing tables, which can only be countered with core router modifications.

Universal Ring

In [115] Castro et al. propose a universal ring, which is based on the Pastry [37] protocol. Peers of all existing overlay networks should participate in the Pastry network, forming a very large common overlay. The universal ring is only used to bootstrap other services, which are being formed separately using grouping mechanisms from Scribe [39]. A trusted authority, e.g. Verisign assigns certificates to a node, such that its node ID is bound with a public key for a certain amount of time. The certification authority should charge nodes for the certificates, to hinder attackers to control many virtual nodes in the universal ring. If there are lots of peers in the universal ring (e.g. through an operating system integration of the protocol), a certified node may try to find the universal ring through random probing or a form of controlled flooding, such as expanding ring IP multicast (see 6.2.1).

6.2.2 Mediator-based approaches

Unlike the peer-based approach, peers using this approach need a special mediator to find other peers of the overlay. The role of the mediator can be played by peers, which are participating in the overlay or by external nodes. Its task comprises of the allocation of a directory service and a *well known entry point* (WKEP), which is hard-coded into the bootstrapping protocol. To join the overlay network, a node then contacts the mediator and requests the address of one or more active peers. One of the major challenges for this kind of approach is to keep the mediator information up to date, such that the directory always contains a list of currently active peers. Furthermore, the accessibility of the mediator is vital to bootstrapping process, as without it, new nodes cannot join the overlay. Some mediator-based approaches have evolved into various products, however only few of them are still in use.

6.2 Bootstrapping

Napster Server

Napster utilizes a directory service to find other peers of the overlay [116]. This service is running on a server farm, which address is hard-coded in the Napster client. The index database stored at Napster contains information about all files that participating peers are willing to share. A peer queries for a certain file and the server answers with an address of a node that shares this file. However, this approach suffers from a single point of failure, as the overlay network is no longer operational if the server farm becomes unavailable. OpenNap [117] tries to eliminate this drawback by allowing each peer to run its own directory server. All of these servers are statically connected and thus only slightly increase the scalability of this approach.

Gnutella Host Caches

The first Gnutella client (namely version 0.4) used a hard-coded URL to discover a bootstrapping server, the so-called *host cache* [3]. A new node connects to the host cache and receives a list of recently active peers, which it then tries to contact. A similar approach was first presented in YOID [118], and later used in CAN [108] and most other recent P2P networks. Whenever the host cache was unreachable, users had to exchange peer addresses manually in chat rooms (e.g. in the IRC). In contrast to the Napster server, the host cache is only needed for the bootstrapping process, but not for the continuous operation of the network. Nevertheless, the host cache depicts a bottleneck in the approach.

The client will then try to establish connections on its own by simply flooding the network with *ping* messages. The neighborhood (up to a hop limit of usually 7) responds with *pong* messages. However, the system therefore suffers from two severe scalability problems. First, the host cache. After Napster was shut down and waves of users logged onto Gnutella, it became obvious that the use of a host cache degrades the network structure. All new users were reported the same recent nodes, which led into a closely clustered network. As packets were dropped on high load situations, users were only able to communicate to their closest neighbors (around 3 hops away) before messages drowned. Second, the flooding mechanism [119] showed that the ping-pong messages made up to 55% of all traffic in a Gnutella network.

Gnutella Host List & Catcher

To improve the efficiency of Gnutella, the bootstrapping process had to make sure that the network cells were not overcrowded. The community solved this problem by manually downloading host lists, which would enforce a sparse network. The client-integrated host catcher records all hosts it encounters during runtime. For future logons, the host list would then be ignored in favor of peers from the host catcher. However, the use of a host catcher entails poor performance, as the lists either have to be reset manually or the client will connect to nodes, which are unfavorable in terms of capacity and topology.

eDonkey Server Lists

To distribute information about active servers in the overlay the eDonkey software utilizes a web-based approach. Users search for a recent *server list*, which they download and integrate in the client. Further updates may then be received over the eDonkey network eliminating the need to download the lists before use of the software. However, companies such as the Recording Industry Association of America (RIAA) try to prevent illegal downloads and thus emit fraudulent information over the update channel. This often renders the service unusable.

Bittorrent

Bittorrent [1] has become one of the most popular file sharing tools, as it allows for clients to upload file fragments among each other (see also Sec. 6.1.3). To start the download of a file, the user has to get a special *.torrent* file, which includes various file information and the URL of the so-called *tracker*. The downloading client informs the tracker about the file it wants to download and on which port it expects further incoming requests. This allows the tracker later to delegate other clients to that node, which then shares the parts it has already downloaded. In doing so, the robustness of the protocol can be severely increased as the original file provider may even leave the network. However, the user still has to search for the torrent file manually and once the tracker is down, new nodes will not be able to download the file.

6.3 Spatial Queries

In this section, we present approaches that allow for spatial queries. These systems provide at least rudimentary support for location-based services on a peer-to-peer basis.

6.3.1 Globase.KOM

The Globase.KOM [14] system offers a P2P overlay for a fully retrievable location-based search. The overlay structure is superpeer-based forming a tree enhanced with interconnections. Each superpeer is responsible for the zone it is in and keeps the contact addresses of other peers. As one zone may contain another zone we get a tree-like structure. The superpeers store contact addresses for the peers in their zone (excluding inner zones), the superpeers of their inner zones, the parent of the tree, the root superpeer and interconnected superpeers. Peers maintain addresses for the parent superpeer, the root superpeer, an interconnection list, and a cache list of already known peers. Once there are too many peers in one zone, the zone gets split and a peer becomes the superpeer for this zone. Crowded locations therefore will face a large tree. In times of high churn the peers at a higher level hence face a high management effort. Their functionality may then become limited due to high loads.

6.3.2 Schmidt's Approach

In [120] the authors present a P2P information discovery system supporting complex searches using keywords. Their system bases on Chord for the overlay network topology and utilizes the Hilbert SFC for the dimension reduction. However, their main focus lies on the mapping of data elements, which are local in a multi-dimensional keyword space, to indices which are local in the 1-dimensional index space. Two documents are considered local, when their keywords are lexicographically close (e.g. computer and computation) or they share common keywords. This comes at a cost, as using space-filling curves does not guarantee a uniform distribution of data elements in the index space. Therefore, additional load-balancing algorithms have to run to reduce the load of heavily used nodes.

6.3.3 Wierum's Approach

Wierum [86] uses a similar index-range metric for comparing the quality of the different curves. However, he intends to use the curves to allow for efficient sorting and searching. Therefore, he only takes the direct neighbors of a zone into account and limits his average error only with regard to those. In our scenario, it is important to find the curve, which minimizes the average error over all zones, as communication will most likely take place between nodes, which are not adjacent.

6.3.4 Palma Project

The Palma Project [121] has dedicated itself to location management using a P2P infrastructure. The goal of this project is to find each node within a certain time span to guarantee the efficient delivery of services to these nodes. The underlying protocol bases on Tapestry and can be adopted to provide fast access to all keys. In highly dynamic environments where mobile nodes use 3G, 4G or wireless LAN technology this problem is far away from being solved. However, there is no relation between where a node is actually located and where its position information is stored. As the project continued [122], the use of security functions made the project dependent of supernodes for authentication. Information is then stored on "stable" servers, which limits its functionality in dynamic environments.

6.3.5 Distributed Space Partitioning Trees

Another interesting approach has been presented by [123] with his work about distributed space partitioning trees (DSPT). The work concentrates on publishing and searching geometrical objects within certain geometrical constraints using a distributed data structure, the DSPT. This data structure is similar to the DHTs, but optimized to handle dynamic geometrical objects. In *RectNet*, a direct implementation of this approach, the first node of the network becomes the so-called clusterhead and is responsible for the entire context space (storing all information and answering all queries locally). As more and more clients enter the area they all send their queries to the clusterhead A, whose load (CPU and traffic) steadily increases. After a certain threshold is exceeded, the clusterhead divides the space into two sub-cluster and has two other nodes (B and C) handle these clusters. As of this moment the clusterhead is responsible for queries surpassing the boundaries of B (or C) forming a tree structure with A as the root and B and C as leaf nodes. Though no leaf node will face load problems as an immediate split of its cluster would occur, the clusterhead will encounter scalability problems as the network grows. This is due to the underlying routing, which forwards all queries from the first sub-cluster to the second sub-cluster over the clusterhead.

6.4 Replication

Existing P2P technologies have various approaches to replication, because of very specific scenarios for which they were designed. To give an overview of replication techniques in P2P technologies, we group the existing approaches into the following classes:

6.4.1 Passive Replication

The main activity in P2P networks is the exchange of data between peers, thereby creating local copies in accordance with the demand. The more popular an object is (that is the more requests for it travel through the network), the more copies of it are found in the network. This process is uncontrolled and cannot be regulated. In this case object-IDs do not necessarily exist in the corresponding location in the P2P ID space, making it difficult to find them in the DHT. Furthermore, a sudden burst of demand for an object can possibly render the *creator* inaccessible, as the replicas do not add to the load-balancing. [124]

6.4.2 Cache-based Replication

In most common P2P protocols intermediate nodes participate in the object transfer and query forwarding [124] process (e.g. routing). These protocols for example include OceanStore [19] and Freenet [18]. Observing passing objects and queries enables the creation of copies of popular objects for caching reasons. This reduces the response time and transfer overhead and may also reduce the load on the original *creator* of the object. One of the major drawbacks of this approach is the fact that a large hop count between two peers nodes will result in replicas on all nodes along the way. This leads to a large storage overhead, which is especially critical at nodes with low storage capacities. Another issue is having a proper policy for the replication management that adapts to traffic changes and determines which objects to keep and which to drop.

6.4.3 Active Content Replication

Active content replication (ACP) was designed to achieve the goal of increasing availability, performance and locality of data. ACP is common, but not limited to unstructured overlays where a non-deterministic search is used. It is used in protocols like Scan [22], Freenet, and Gnutella [3], where it is also known as dynamic or proactive replication. Scan applies the smart dynamic replication strategy, which performs best in terms of bandwidth consumption. The Gnutella protocol [21, 68] had a rather statistical approach to assign replication weights to each node. Comparing P2P network performance in case of uniform replication on one hand and linearly proportional replication related to popularity on the other hand, the replication designers have concluded that an intermediate solution through proportional square-root replication will achieve best performance and least replication overhead [125]. The focus of ACP however lies on unstructured overlays and is hard to implement in DHT-based systems.

6.4.4 OceanStore's Replica Management

OceanStore, a distributed storage architecture built on Tapestry [126], uses intelligent replication management to keep efficient and consistent storage and versioning services. At the same time, it uses security mechanisms to keep object integrity and provide secure access to data.

The focus of OceanStore is on the persistence of data i.e. preventing data loss. However, it does not provide mechanisms to dynamically adapt to changing request rates. Each version of data is stored in a read-only form, which is encoded using erasure-codes and then spread over thousands of servers. In a flash-crowd scenario, OceanStore produces high costs for the generation of these erasure-encoded fragments. To satisfy the requests the consistency restrictions may be lowered, however clients will receive older versions then. Additionally, the created fragments cause

6.4 Replication

an overhead through the additionally needed storage [127], thereby violating the efficiency requirement.

6.4.5 PAST's Initial Factor Assignment

PAST [40] uses location randomization to place copies of its replicas. This results in geographically diverse locations and ownerships for replicas. PAST differs from the other protocols in adding an initial replication factor k to each object. This factor depends on the estimated availability and persistence requirements for a certain object. The k peers having the closest ID to the most significant bits of the object identifier shall maintain replicas of this object. However, the assignment of an initial factor at the insertion time poses to be the drawback of this schema as it is not able to consider future changes for an object's popularity.

6.4.6 Static Replication Schemes

Several approaches tried to increase their robustness through means of replication. However, they do not take a single data element into account, but rather set the level of replication degree at the initialization. Therefore, they too are not able to cope with peaks in the interest of a specific data element.

Chord

Chord [20] - not providing a replication by itself - however does provide an infrastructure suitable for replication. These successor lists contain the nodes succeeding the peer's key. The application using the replication can decide on the amount of entries it needs. According to the protocol, the node keeps track of these nodes and update the successor lists as they join and leave the network. This allows for a simple replication of data to the peers in the successor list, however without any geographic relation.

CAN

CAN [108] is another well-analyzed P2P system. In CAN, the ID space is divided in so-called zones, where there is at least one peer per zone. CAN offers two mechanisms, which can be exploited for replication. On the one hand, CAN supports realities, allowing in each reality a different peer is responsible for a certain piece of information. On the other hand, CAN can be configured such that it allows multiple peers in one zone, each one responsible for the same data. Though this procedure allows for load-balancing, it is not dynamic and lacks mechanisms to minimize the effect of peaks.

Chapter 7

Conclusion

As peer-to-peer systems emerge in more and more scenarios, new challenges will keep coming up and require our attention. With this work we faced three of those challenges, namely providing an automated bootstrapping protocol to set up a P2P-overlay network, dealing with location-based information and increasing the availability for highly requested information through means of replication. Our contributions to the field enable developers to build their own peer-to-peer applications and share information efficiently, making them suitable for a variety of application fields.

Firstly, we have presented a novel approach for an automated bootstrapping protocol for P2P-systems (see Section 3.3). To achieve this, we have used existing Internet technologies, such as the Dynamic Domain Name Service (DDNS) and the Internet Relay Chat (IRC). Those services are highly distributed and thus supply the robustness and availability needed to provide a successful bootstrap in absence of a central authority. Furthermore, we have developed the concept of "Guardians". Thereby, we extended our bootstrapping scheme to offer resilience against multiple simultaneous node failures while keeping the load on the used Internet service (DDNS and IRC) very low.

Secondly, we have proposed an architecture for hosting context-based information on a peer-to-peer basis. In contrast to existing location-based systems [7–9] our algorithm optimizes the data distribution towards geographic locality, keeping the distance information travels short. We have run simulations with space-filling curves, such that we could evaluate small-world scenarios (see Section 4.4). Through the simulations, we showed that the Hilbert curve possesses superior locality properties.

To facilitate the mapping between Earth and the Hilbert curve, we apply the Peirce projection on the geoid and then put the curve on top of the 2D map. Thus, the user is able to pick an arbitrary point or region on the map and calculate the appropriate Hilbert index on the curve. With this index, the user is able to compute the according node ID (position) respectively node IDs (region) of the peers that are responsible for this location. In the following, the user may send spatial queries with the calculated node ID as a target key. The adapted prefix routing from Pastry [37] in combination with Geostry's locality optimizations makes sure the query reaches the closest active peer to the desired location. Thus, our system is able to cope with all kinds of spatial queries (see Section 2.4.2) and delivers the best possible functionality for a location-based system.

Lastly, we have developed an efficient replication scheme in a location-based peer-to-peer network. Therefore, we studied replication methods, which backup the data on nearby nodes, so that in case a node disconnects from the ring, the information stored on that node will still be available in the same region. This is especially reasonable as a majority of requests for a certain piece of geographic-related information arrives from the immediate vicinity [106]. In Section 5.4, we presented our replication design for efficient replication algorithm also being capable of handling highly dynamic data. Furthermore, we enhanced this scheme to provide resilience in times of high loads caused by so-called flash-crowds. This is done through the replication of the highly requested data to nearby (in terms of geography) peers and to well-known addresses at remote spots.

Using the results from this work, users may setup their own peer-to-peer applications, have other users join their network to exchange location-based information and even provide high availability in case some piece of information "gets hot". Thereby, we fulfill all the requirements for the Geostry process in Section 1.1.

Future Research Activities

Even though Geostry provides all means for creating a P2P application, dealing with location-based data and providing appropriate means of replication, some open research questions still remain. Several ideas might seem far fetched, but we are sure that the following aspects are worthwhile investigating.

In Section 3.3, we have presented our novel bootstrapping approach. The focus of this approach lies on the technical feasibility rather than on security aspects. As most DDNS accounts are protected by a password, the challenge how the password is guarded remains subject to future research. In addition, the list of the nodes from the node cache should be validated to hinder malicious nodes to distribute their own "fake" node lists. This could be achieved by a majority voting of all the nodes in the overlay, simulating a simple intrusion detection system (IDS). For as long as $(n+1)/2$ peers share a valid node list, malicious nodes could be detected and newly added peers eventually join the "correct" overlay and receive a valid node list.

Another interesting task is the assignment of node IDs. In Section 4.5, we have demonstrated our node ID assignment scheme basing on the node's current position. By enhancing this approach through a third dimension we can classify the peers by the major topic they are offering. However, some nodes may provide information covering several topics. This requires a node to register itself at several locations in the overlay. However, this may lead to an increase in management tasks (keeping lists up-to-date etc.). It is conceivable, that the peer reduces the amount of connections and the update intervals to other peer in relation to the amount of topics it wants to cover to cope with this problem. Nevertheless, such problems were out of scope of this work.

Our proposed replication scheme from Section 5.4 outlined how to deal with information that gets heavily requested. Through our multi-stage approach, a peer might have to send a query several times until it learns (through time-outs) of the creator's state and thus re-sends the query to a peer at a well-known remote location. "Impatient" peers need the information as soon as possible. It is therefore imaginable, that the querying peer sends several queries simultaneously to eventually get an answer without waiting for an answer from the first peer. It would be an interesting task to apply an exponential back-off that grows with the distance to the creator.

Appendix A

Peirce Projection

The formulas for the Peirce projection are taken from the United States Coast Survey [128] and a private conversation with Carlos Furuti [60].

A.1 Projecting Geographical Coordinates

In the following, we describe the transformation for coordinates from a geographical reference system to the domain of the Peirce coordinates.

Given: latitude phi (ϕ), longitude lambda (λ)
Auxiliary variables: a,b,n,m

$$\cos a = \frac{\cos\phi(\sin\lambda + \cos\phi)}{\sqrt{2}} \tag{A.1}$$

$$\cos b = \frac{\cos\phi(\sin\lambda - \cos\phi)}{\sqrt{2}} \tag{A.2}$$

$$\sin m = \pm\sqrt{1 + \cos a \cos b - \sin a \sin b} \tag{A.3}$$

$$\sin n = \pm\sqrt{1 - \cos a \cos b - \sin a \sin b} \tag{A.4}$$

$$x = \int_0^m \sqrt{1 - \frac{\sin^2 m}{2}}\, dm \tag{A.5}$$

$$y = \int_0^n \sqrt{1 - \frac{\sin^2 n}{2}}\, dn \tag{A.6}$$

The sign in formula $A.3$ is inverted if $180°\mathrm{W} \leq \lambda \leq 0°\mathrm{W}$
The sign in formula $A.4$ is inverted if $90°\mathrm{W} \leq \lambda \leq 90°\mathrm{E}$.

The equations above are only valid for $0° \leq \phi \leq 90°$N.
The southern hemisphere is similar and symmetric, however interrupted.

A.1.1 Solving the Equations

Evaluating the integrals numerically can be achieved using a mathematical tool, such as Maple [129] or Mathematica [130]. Using those we get a combination of complete and incomplete elliptic functions depending in the magnitude mg of the argument. Evaluating few numerical values for the argument, we see that the "switch" from the single elliptic function to the combination of two occurs at $\frac{\Pi}{2}$. [100] show how the results can be combined into a single equation named PP (see Algorithm A.7). The domain for the projected image can be derived from elliptic function EllitpticF in Fig. A.1. The maximum and the minimum of the function can then be calculated using the limit as shown in Formula A.8 and A.9. For further information about elliptic integrals please consult further resources (e.g. [131]).

$$PP(mg) = \begin{cases} 2EllipticK(\frac{1}{2}\sqrt{2}) - EllipticF(\sin(|mg|), \frac{1}{2}\sqrt{2}), & \text{if } mg > \frac{\pi}{2} \\ EllipticF(\sin(|mg|), \frac{1}{2}\sqrt{2}), & \text{otherwise} \end{cases} \quad (A.7)$$

$$\lim_{mg \to \frac{\Pi}{2}} EllipticF(\sin(|mg|), \frac{1}{2}\sqrt{2}) = 1.854 \quad (A.8)$$

$$\lim_{mg \to \frac{3\Pi}{2}} EllipticF(\sin(|mg|), \frac{1}{2}\sqrt{2}) = -1.854 \quad (A.9)$$

A.2 Calculating the Index on the Hilbert Curve

For spatial queries (e.g. position queries) we need to define a POI on a map and derive the appropriate indexes on the space-filling curve. We use HilbertIndex to calculate the index for a given geographic coordinate.

A.2 Calculating the Index on the Hilbert Curve

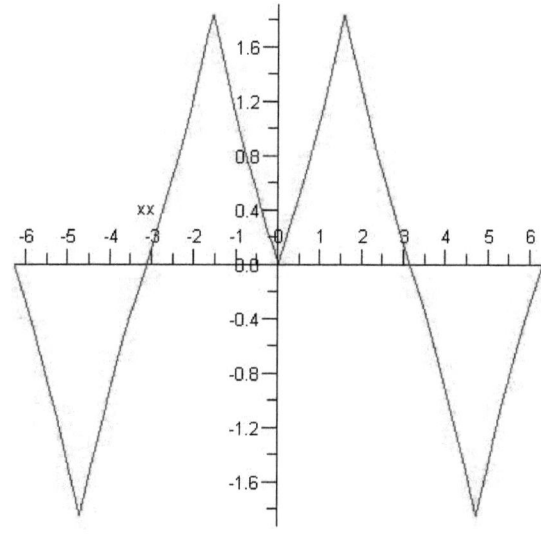

Figure A.1: The progression of the elliptic integral of the first kind

Algorithm 12 Calculate Hilbert Index
1: **function** HilbertIndex(x, y, $order$)
2:   xc = 2 * floor(x) + 1
3:   yc = 2 * floor(y) + 1
4:   **return** HIndex(xc, yc, $order$)

Algorithm 13 HilbertIndex: Main Loop

1: **function** HIndex(x, y, $order$)
2:   **if** order == 0 **then**
3:     **return** 0;
4:   **end if**
5:   **if** x < (2^{order}) **then**
6:     **if** y < (2^{order}) **then**
7:       **return** 0 * ($4^{order-1}$) + HIndex(y,x, order - 1);
8:     **else**
9:       **return** 1 * ($4^{order-1}$) + HIndex(x,y - (2^{order}), order - 1);
10:     **end if**
11:   **else**
12:     **if** y < (2^{order}) **then**
13:       **return** 3 * ($4^{order-1}$) + HIndex((2^{order}) - y, ($2^{order+1}$) - x, order - 1);
14:     **else**
15:       **return** 2 * ($4^{order-1}$) + HIndex(x - (2^{order}), y - (2^{order}), order - 1);
16:     **end if**
17:   **end if**

Glossary

Azimuth Given a reference point R and two other points S_1 and S_2 on a surface, the azimuth from S_1 to S_2 is the angle formed by the minimum-distance lines (Great Circle Paths) RS_1 and RS_2. 43

Fractal In general, a fractal is a "rough or fragmented geometric shape that can be split into parts, each of which is (at least approximately) a reduced-size copy of the whole" [132]. This property is called *self-similarity*. 35

Geoid (greek for earth-shaped) There is no simple geometric shape that matches Earth. Furthermore, the surface is not smooth, which further complicates the shape. Earth's shape therefore is called geoid. 36

Great Circle Paths also called *geodetic* or *orthodrome lines* represent the shortest path between any two points. Additionally, they are also centered on the sphere. 42, 129

LBS (short for Location-based Service) are services providing selected information to the end-user. This presented data may depend on the current location, time, or the user's preferences. 2

Locality In contrast to other P2P systems Pastry takes locality into account. In the underlying Internet it seeks to minimize the distance messages travel according to a scalar proximity metric (e.g. ping delay). 20

Meridian All joining points of the same longitude are called meridians. The meridians are halves of circles, which are converging in the north and south poles. Therefore, they cannot be regarded as parallels. 38

Replication The word derives from biology, where the term *replication* is used for the reproduction of living cells. In computer terms the word may refer to duplication of information in hard disks (e.g. RAID), Databases or Networks. 94

Bibliography

[1] B. Cohen, "Incentives build robustness in bittorrent," in *In Proceedings of the First Workshop on the Economics of Peer-to-Peer Systems*, Berkeley, CA, USA, June 2003. [Online]. Available: http://citeseer.ist.psu.edu/cohen03incentives.html

[2] M. Falck, "Das deutsche emule portal," http://www.emule.de, 2006. [Online]. Available: http://www.emule.de

[3] G. Kan, "Gnutella," in *Peer-to-Peer. Harnessing the Power of Disruptive Technologies*, A. Oram, Ed.   Sebastopol, CA, USA: O'Reilly, 2001, pp. 94–122.

[4] Cachelogic, "Internet traffic study 2004," June 2004. [Online]. Available: http://www.cachelogic.com/home/pages/studies/2004_01.php

[5] J. Liang, R. Kumar, and K. W. Ross, "Understanding kazaa," Polytechnic University, New York, USA, Tech. Rep., May 2004. [Online]. Available: http://cis.poly.edu/~ross/papers/UnderstandingKaZaA.pdf.

[6] "le site lugdunum," http://lugdunum2k.free.fr/id.html, 2005, in French. [Online]. Available: http://lugdunum2k.free.fr/id.html

[7] D. Dudkowski and T. Schwarz, "The neXus Homepage," http://www.nexus.uni-stuttgart.de, 2005. [Online]. Available: http://www.nexus.uni-stuttgart.de

[8] Hewlett-Packard, "Cooltown," 2008. [Online]. Available: http://www.cooltown.com/cooltownhome/index.asp

[9] C. Kidd, R. Orr, G. Abowd, C. Atkeson, I. Essa, B. MacIntyre, E. Mynatt, T. Starner, and W. Newstetter, "The Aware Home: A Living Laboratory for Ubiquitous Computing Research," in *Second International Workshop on Cooperative Buildings*.   Springer, 1999, pp. 191–198.

[10] D. S. Milojicic, V. Kalogeraki, R. Lukose, K. Nagaraja, J. Pruyne, B. Richard, S. Rollins, and Z. Xu, "Peer-to-Peer Computing," HP Laboratories Palo Alto, Tech. Rep. HPL-2002-57, March 2002. [Online]. Available: citeseer.ist.psu.edu/milojicic02peertopeer.html

[11] M. Hauswirth and S. Dustdar, "Peer-to-Peer: Grundlagen und Architektur," *Datenbank-Spektrum*, vol. 13, pp. 5–13, May 2005, (in German).

[12] Y. Chawathe, S. Ramabhadran, S. Ratnasamy, A. LaMarca, S. Shenker, and J. Hellerstein, "A case study in building layered dht applications," *SIGCOMM Comput. Commun. Rev.*, vol. 35, no. 4, pp. 97–108, 2005.

[13] S. Zhou, G. R. Ganger, and P. Steenkiste, "Location-based node ids: Enabling explicit locality in dhts," Computer Science Department, Carnegie Mellon University, Tech. Rep., 2003.

[14] A. Kovacevic, N. Liebau, and R. Steinmetz, "Globase.kom - a p2p overlay for fully retrievable location-based search," in *Proceedings of the Seventh IEEE International Conference on Peer-to-Peer Computing*, September 2007.

[15] A. Harwood and E. Tanin, "Hashing spatial content over peer-to-peer networks," in *In Australian Telecommunications, Networks, and Applications Conference-ATNAC*, 2003.

[16] A. Mondal, Y. Lifu, and M. Kitsuregawa, "P2pr-tree: An r-tree-based spatial index for peer-to-peer environments," *Current Trends in Database Technology - EDBT 2004 Workshops*, pp. 516–525, 2004. [Online]. Available: http://www.springerlink.com/content/9r6wl93g52bg6c75

[17] T. Mann, A. Hisgen, and G. Swart, "An algorithm for data replication," Systems Research Center (SRC) at Digital Equipment Corporation (DEC), Tech. Rep., 1989.

[18] I. Clarke, O. Sandberg, B. Wiley, and T. W. Hong, "Freenet: A distributed anonymous information storage and retrieval system," *Lecture Notes in Computer Science*, vol. 2009, p. 46ff., 2001. [Online]. Available: citeseer.ist.psu.edu/clarke00freenet.html

[19] J. Kubiatowicz, D. Bindel, Y. Chen, P. Eaton, D. Geels, R. Gummadi, S. Rhea, H. Weatherspoon, W. Weimer, C. Wells, and B. Zhao, "OceanStore: An Architecture for Global-scale Persistent Storage," in *Proceedings of ACM ASPLOS*. ACM, November 2000. [Online]. Available: citeseer.ist.psu.edu/kubiatowicz00oceanstore.html

[20] I. Stoica, R. Morris, D. Karger, M. F. Kaashoek, and H. Balakrishnan, "Chord: A scalable peer-to-peer lookup service for internet applications," in *SIGCOMM '01: Proceedings of the 2001 conference on Applications, technologies, architectures, and protocols for computer communications*. San Diego, CA, USA: ACM Press, 2001, pp. 149–160.

[21] S. Saroiu, P. K. Gummadi, and S. D. Gribble, "A measurement study of peer-to-peer file sharing systems," in *SPIE/ACM Conference on Multimedia Computing and Networking (MMCN) 2002*, San Jose, CA, USA, January 18-25 2002. [Online]. Available: citeseer.ist.psu.edu/saroiu02measurement.html

[22] Y. Chen, R. H. Katz, and J. D. Kubiatowicz, "Scan: A dynamic, scalable and efficient content distribution network," *Lecture Notes in Computer Science*, vol. 2414, pp. 145–148, 2002.

[23] Dynamic Network Services, Inc., "The DynDNS Homepage," September 2007. [Online]. Available: http://www.dyndns.org

[24] A. Oram, "Peer-to-peer makes the internet interesting again," O'Reilly's openp2p.com, 22nd September 2000. [Online]. Available: http://www.linuxdevcenter.com/pub/a/linux/2000/09/22/p2psummit.html

[25] B. Loban, "Between rhizomes and trees: P2p information systems," *first monday*, vol. 9, no. 10, October 2004. [Online]. Available: http://firstmonday.org/issues/issue9_10/loban/index.html

[26] "The seti@home faq," September 2008. [Online]. Available: http://seticlassic.ssl.berkeley.edu/faq.html#q1.21

[27] A. International, "China: Internet companies assist censorship," Press Release (AI Index: ASA 17/002/2006), 25th January 2006. [Online]. Available: http://www.amnesty.org/en/library/asset/ASA17/002/2006/en/dom-ASA170022006en.html

[28] "Google products," September 2008. [Online]. Available: http://www.google.com/intl/en/options

[29] I. Clarke, "The Free Network Project," August 2008. [Online]. Available: http://freenetproject.org/news.html?lang=en

[30] Clip2 / Gnutella Developer Forum, "The Gnutella Protocol v0.4," http://groups.yahoo.com/group/thegdf/files/Development, 2001. [Online]. Available: http://groups.yahoo.com/group/the_gdf/files/Development/

[31] J. Liang, R. Kumarb, and K. W. Ross, "The fasttrack overlay: A measurement study," *Computer Networks: The International Journal of Computer and Telecommunications Networking*, vol. 50, no. 6, pp. 842–858, April 2006.

[32] R. Steinmetz and K. Wehrle, *Peer-to-Peer Systems and Applications*. Springer, 2005.

[33] "The Napster Homepage," http://www.napster.com, 2005. [Online]. Available: http://www.napster.com

[34] V. Rijmen and E. Oswald, "Update on sha-1," in *The Cryptographers' Track at the RSA Conference 2005*, vol. 3376. San Francisco, CA, USA: Springer, February 14-18 2005, pp. 58–71. [Online]. Available: http://www.springerlink.com/content/ryl16lh797w4xb34/

[35] I. Clarke, S. G. Miller, T. W. Hong, O. Sandberg, and B. Wiley, "Protecting free expression online with freenet," *IEEE Internet Computing*, vol. 6, no. 1, pp. 40–49, 2002.

[36] J. Ahola. (2008, August) P2P Next: Shaping the Next Generation of Internet TV. [Online]. Available: http://www.p2p-next.org/

[37] A. Rowstron and P. Druschel, "Pastry: Scalable, distributed object loaction for routing for large-scale peer-to-peer systems," in *Proceedings IFIP/ACM Middleware 2001*, Heidelberg, Germany, November 2001.

[38] M. Castro, P. Druschel, A.-M. Kermarrec, A. Nandi, A. Rowstron, and A. Singh, "Splitstream: high-bandwidth multicast in cooperative environments," in *SOSP '03: Proceedings of the nineteenth ACM symposium on Operating systems principles*. New York, NY, USA: ACM Press, October 2003, pp. 298–313.

[39] M. Castro, P. Druschel, A. Kermarrec, and A. Rowstron, "Scribe: a large-scale and decentralized application-level multicast infrastructure," *IEEE Journal on Selected Areas in Communications*, vol. 20, no. 8, pp. 1489–1499, October 2002.

[40] A. Rowstron and P. Druschel, "Storage management and caching in past, a large-scale, persistent peer-to-peer storage utility," in *18th ACM SOSP*, Lake Louise, Alberta, Canada, October 2001.

[41] K. M. Hansen, "P2P Storage," November 25 2003. [Online]. Available: http://www.daimi.au.dk/~marius/p2p-course/lectures/11/talk.html

[42] C. Cramer, K. Kutzner, and T. Fuhrmann, "Bootstrapping locality-aware p2p networks," in *Proceedings of the IEEE International Conference on Networks (ICON)*, Singapore, November 2004, publication, pp. 357–361. [Online]. Available: http://i30www.ira.uka.de/research/publications/p2p/

[43] H. Ballani and P. Francis, "Towards a Deployable IP Anycast Service," in *Proc. of First Workshop on Real, Large Distributed Systems (WORLDS '04)*, December 2004.

[44] J. Samsioe and A. Samsioe, *Mobile Kommunikation: Wertschöpfung, Technologien, neue Dienste*. Gabler Verlag, 2002, ch. Introduction to Location Based Services - Markets and Technologies.

[45] B. Schilit, N. Adams, and R. Want, "Context-aware computing applications," in *In Proceedings of the Workshop on Mobile Computing Systems and Applications*. IEEE Computer Society, 1994, pp. 85–90.

[46] A. Schmidt, M. Beigl, and H.-W. Gellersen, "There is more to context than location," *Computers and Graphics*, vol. 23, no. 6, pp. 893–901, 1999.

[47] K. Rothermel, M. Bauer, and C. Becker, *Digitale Weltmodelle - Grundlage kontextbezogener Systeme*, F. Mattern, Ed. Springer, 2003.

[48] C. Becker, "System support for context-aware computing," Professorial Dissertation, June 2004, university of Stuttgart.

[49] S. Domnitcheva, "Location modeling: State of the art and challenges," in *Proceedings of the 2001 Workshop on Location Modeling for Ubiquitous Computing (UbiComp 2001)*, Atlanta, GA, USA, 2001, pp. 13–20.

[50] U. Leonhardt, "Supporting location-awareness in open distributed systems," Ph.D. dissertation, Department of Computing, Imperial College, London, UK, 1998.

[51] K. Bolino, "Cartesian coordinate system," Wikimedia Commons (Public Domain), September 2008. [Online]. Available: http://en.wikipedia.org/wiki/File:Cartesian-coordinate-system.svg

[52] Ekahau, "Wi-fi based real-time tracking," February 2009. [Online]. Available: http://www.ekahau.com

[53] R. J. Orr and G. D. Abowd, "The smart floor: a mechanism for natural user identification and tracking," in *CHI '00: CHI '00 extended abstracts on Human factors in computing systems*. New York, NY, USA: ACM, 2000, pp. 275–276.

[54] M. Bader, *Algorithmen des Wissenschaftlichen Rechnens*, Technical University Munich, 23rd May 2005.

[55] H. Sagan, *Space-Filling Curves*, J. Ewing, F. Gehring, and P. Halmos, Eds. New York, NY, USA: Springer-Verlag, 1994.

[56] E. Netto, "Beitrag zur Mannigfaltigkeitslehre," *Journal für die reine und angewandte Mathematik*, vol. 86, pp. 263–268, 1879.

[57] G. Rozenberg and A. Salomaa, *The mathematical theory of L systems*. New York, USA: Academic Press, 1980.

[58] D. G. Bobrow, "Berkeley logo," September 2008. [Online]. Available: http://www.cs.berkeley.edu/~bh/logo.html

[59] B. Nielsen, "Lindenmayer systemer," http://www.246.dk/lsystems.html, March 2006, (in Danish). [Online]. Available: http://www.246.dk/lsystems.html

[60] C. A. Furuti, "Map projections," http://www.progonos.com/furuti/MapProj/CartIndex/cartIndex.html, May 2006. [Online]. Available: http://www.progonos.com/furuti/MapProj/CartIndex/cartIndex.html

[61] K. Wagner, *Karthographische Netzentwürfe*. Karlsruhe, Germany: Herbert Wichmann Verlag, 1983.

[62] D. G. Milbert and D. A. Smith, "Converting gps height into navd88 elevation with the geoid96 geoid height model," 1996. [Online]. Available: http://www.ngs.noaa.gov/PUBS_LIB/gislis96.html

[63] Ttog, "Geographic coordinates on a sphere," Wikimedia Commons (Creative Commons Attribution ShareAlike 3.0), June 2006. [Online]. Available: http://de.wikipedia.org/w/index.php?title=Datei:Geographic_coordinates_sphere.svg&filetimestamp=20060629215155

[64] Traroth, "Schéma illustrant des projections," Wikimedia Commons (GNU Free Documentation License), March 22nd 2005.

[65] R. Böhm, "Vimage v4.1.250," Ingenieurbüro fr Kartograhie Bad Schandau, August 2008. [Online]. Available: http://www.boehmwanderkarten.de/kartographie/is_netze_projection_vimage_tutorial.html

[66] A. S. Tanenbaum and M. van Steen, *Verteilte Systeme*. Pearson Studium, 2007.

[67] G. Coulouris, J. Dollimore, and T. Kindberg, *Verteilte Systeme*, 3rd ed. Addison Wesley, 2002.

[68] P. Kirk, "The annotated gnutella protocol specification v0.4," 2003. [Online]. Available: http://rfc-gnutella.sourceforge.net/developer/stable/index.html

[69] Q. Lv, P. Cao, E. Cohen, K. Li, and S. Shenker, "Search and replication in unstructured peer-to-peer networks," in *ICS '02: Proceedings of the 16th international conference on Supercomputing*. New York, NY, USA: ACM, 2002, pp. 84–95.

[70] M. Knoll, A. Wacker, G. Schiele, and T. Weis, "Decentralized bootstrapping in pervasive applications," *Fifth Annual IEEE International Conference on Pervasive Computing and Communications Workshops (PerComW'07)*, pp. 589–592, 2007.

[71] C. Cramer and T. Fuhrmann, "Bootstrapping chord in ad hoc networks: Not going anywhere for a while," in *Proceedings of the 3rd IEEE International Workshop on Mobile Peer-to-Peer Computing*, Pisa, Italy, March 2006, publication. [Online]. Available: http://i30www.ira.uka.de/research/publications/p2p/

[72] W. Ding, "Bootstrapping chord over manets - all roads lead to rome," in *IEEE Wireless Communications and Networking Conference (WCNC)*, Kowloon, China, March 11-15 2007, pp. 3501–3506.

[73] J. Oikarinen and D. Reed, "Internet relay chat protocol," Internet Network Working Group RFC 1459, May 1993.

[74] Z. Wang and X. Yang, *Birth and death processes and Markov chains*. Beijing, China: Science Press, 1992.

[75] G. Schiele, R. Sueselbeck, A. Wacker, J. Haehner, C. Becker, and T. Weis, "Requirements of peer-to-peer-based massively multiplayer online gaming," in *Proceedings of the Seventh International Workshop on Global and Peer-to-Peer Computing*, 2007.

[76] T. Moore and R. Clayton, "An empirical analysis of the current state of phishing attack and defence," in *Sixth Workshop on the Economics of Information Security*, June 7-8 2007. [Online]. Available: http://www.cl.cam.ac.uk/~twm29/weis07-phishing.pdf

[77] The Honeynet Project & Research Alliance, "Fast-flux service networks: An ever changing enemy," July 13th 2007. [Online]. Available: http://www.honeynet.org/papers/ff/fast-flux.html

[78] R. Porter and Y. Shoham, "Addressing the Free-Rider Roblem in File-Sharing Systems: A Mechanism-Design Approach," in *In Proceedings of EC'04*, New York, NY, USA, 2004.

[79] O. Lehmann, M. Bauer, C. Becker, and D. Nicklas, "From home to world - supporting context-aware applications through world models," in *PERCOM '04: Proceedings of the Second IEEE International Conference on Pervasive Computing and Communications (PerCom'04)*. Washington, DC, USA: IEEE Computer Society, 2004, p. 297.

[80] M. Grossmann, M. Bauer, N. Hönle, U.-P. Käppeler, D. Nicklas, and T. Schwarz, "Efficiently Managing Context Information for Large-scale Scenarios," in *Proceedings of the 3rd IEEE Conference on Pervasive Computing and Communications (PerCom2005)*. IEEE Computer Society, March 2005.

[81] Sesmith, "All colonies blank map," Wikimedia Commons (Public Domain), Aug 2009. [Online]. Available: http://commons.wikimedia.org/wiki/File:All_colonies_blank_map.png

[82] M. Knoll and T. Weis, "A P2P-Framework for Context-based Information," in *1st International Workshop on Requirements and Solutions for Pervasive Software Infrastructures (RSPSI) at Pervasive 2006*, Dublin, Ireland, May 2006.

[83] C. Gotsman and M. Lindenbaum, "On the metric properties of discrete space-filling curves," *IEEE Transactions of Image Processing*, vol. 5, no. 5, May 1996.

[84] H. V. Jagadish, "Linear clustering of objects with multiple attributes," *SIGMOD Rec.*, vol. 19, no. 2, pp. 332–342, 1990.

[85] R. Niedermeier, K. Reinhardt, and P. Sanders, "Towards optimal locality in mesh-indexings," in *Fundamentals of Computation Theory*, 1997, pp. 364–375. [Online]. Available: citeseer.ist.psu.edu/article/niedermeier97towards.html

[86] J.-M. Wierum, "Logarithmic path-length in space-filling curves," in *Proceedings of the 14th Canadian Conference on Computational Geometry*, S. Wismath, Ed., Lethbridge, August 2002, pp. 22–26.

[87] Manifold Net Ltd., "The manifold.net homepage," October 2008. [Online]. Available: http://www.manifold.net

[88] J. P. Snyder, *Flattening the Earth: Two Thousand Years of Map Projections*. Chicago, IL, USA: University of Chicago Press, October 1st 1993.

[89] D. M. German, P. d'Angelo, M. Gross, and B. Postle, "New methods to project panoramas for practical and aesthetic purposes," in *Computational Aestethics in Graphics, Visualization, and Imaging (CAe 2007)*, D. W. Cunningham, G. Meyer, L. Neumann, A. Dunning, and R. Paricio, Eds. Eurographics Association, June 2007, pp. 13–22.

[90] C. S. Peirce, "A quincuncial projection of the sphere," *American Journal of Mathematics*, vol. 2, no. 4, pp. 394–396, 1879. [Online]. Available: http://www.jstor.org/stable/2369491

[91] M. Pögl, "Entwicklung eines cache-optimalen 3D Finite-Elemente-Verfahrens für große Probleme," Ph.D. dissertation, Technische Universität München, Munich, Germany, 2004.

[92] H.-O. Peitgen and D. Saupe, Eds., *The Science of Fractal Images*. New York, NY, USA: Springer-Verlag, 1988.

[93] M. Alfonseca and A. Ortega, "Representation of fractal curves by means of l systems," in *APL '96: Proceedings of the conference on Designing the future*. New York, NY, USA: ACM Press, 1996, pp. 13–21.

[94] H. Abelson and A. diSessa, *Turtle Geometry: The Computer as a Medium for Exploring Mathematics*. Cambridge, MA, USA: The MIT Press, 1981.

[95] P. A. Tipler, G. Mosca, and D. Pelte, *Physik*, 2nd ed. Spektrum Akademischer Verlag, 2004, (in German).

[96] M. W. Gutowski, "Smooth genetic algorithm," *Journal of Physics A: Mathematical and General*, vol. 27, no. 23, December 1994.

[97] D. J. Watts and S. H. Strogatz, "Collective dynamics of small-world networks," *Nature*, vol. 393, no. 6, pp. 440–442, 1998.

[98] D. J. Watts, *Small Worlds*. Princeton, NJ, USA: Princeton University Press, 1999.

[99] P. Hogan, "Nasa world wind," January 2008. [Online]. Available: http://worldwind.arc.nasa.gov

[100] R. Taylor, R. Baur, and J. Oprea, "Maple maps," January 2008. [Online]. Available: http://people.clarkson.edu/~chengweb/faculty/taylor/maps/maps1.html

[101] G. Mealy, "A method for synthesizing sequential circuits," *Bell System Tech Journal*, vol. 34, pp. 1045–1079, 1955.

[102] R. Dickau, "Hilbert and morre 3d fractal curves," The Wolfram Demonstration Project, 2008.

[103] J. Elson and J. Howell, "Handling flash crowds from your garage," in *USENIX Annual Technical Conference*, 2008. [Online]. Available: http://www.usenix.org/events/usenix08/tech/full_papers/elson/elson_html/index.html

[104] The Slashdot Homepage, "What is the slashdot effect?" June 2000. [Online]. Available: http://slashdot.org/faq/slashmeta.shtml

[105] H. G. Sanjay Ghemawat and S.-T. Leung, "The google filesystem," in *19th ACM Symposium on Operating Systems Principles*, Lake George, NY. USA, October 2003.

[106] B. Xu, A. Ouksel, and O. Wolfson, "Opportunistic resource exchange in inter-vehicle ad hoc networks," in *Proc. of the Fifth IEEE International Conference on Mobile Data Management (MDM)*, Berkeley, CA, USA, January 2004, pp. 4–12.

[107] Mirko Knoll and Torben Weis, "Optimizing Locality for Self-organizing Context-Based Systems," in *International Workshop on Self-Organizing Systems (IWSOS 2006)*. Passau, Germany: Springer, September 18-20 2006.

[108] S. Ratnasamy, P. Francis, M. Handley, R. Karp, and S. Shenker, "A scalable content-addressable network," in *Proceedings of the 2001 Conference on Applications, Technologies, Architectures, and Protocols for Computer Communications (SIGCOMM)*. San Diego, CA, USA: ACM Press, 2001, pp. 161–172.

[109] S. P. Ratnasamy, "A Scaleable Content-Adressable Network," Ph.D. dissertation, University of California, Berkeley, CA, USA, 2002.

[110] J. Kubiatowicz, "The OceanStore Project," http://oceanstore.cs.berkeley.edu/, November 2005. [Online]. Available: http://oceanstore.cs.berkeley.edu/

[111] J. A. Pouwelse, P. Garbacki, D. Epema, and H. Sips, "The Bittorrent P2P File-Sharing System: Measurements and Analysis," in *4th International Workshop on Peer-To-Peer Systems*. Springer Verlag, February 2005, cornell University Campus, Ithaca, New York, USA. [Online]. Available: http://iptps05.cs.cornell.edu/PDFs/CameraReady_202.pdf

[112] C. Gkantsidis and P. R. Rodriguez, "Avalanche: Network coding for large scale content distribution," in *IEEE Infocom*, 2005.

[113] L. N. Foner, "Political artifacts and personal privacy: The yenta multi-agent distributed matchmaking system," Ph.D. dissertation, Massachusetts Institure of Technology, April 1999.

[114] J. Abley, A. Canada, and K. Lindqvist, "Operation of anycast services," Request for Comments: 4786 / Best Current Practice: 126, December 2006. [Online]. Available: http://www.ietf.org/rfc/rfc4786.txt

[115] M. Castro, P. Druschel, A.-M. Kermarrec, and A. Rowstron, "One ring to rule them all: service discovery and binding in structured peer-to-peer overlay networks," in *EW10: Proceedings of the 10th workshop on ACM SIGOPS European workshop: beyond the PC*. New York, NY, USA: ACM Press, 2002, pp. 140–145.

Bibliography

[116] C. Shirky, "Listening to napster," in *Peer-to-Peer. Harnessing the Power of Disruptive Technologies*, A. Oram, Ed. Sebastopol, CA, USA: O'Reilly, 2001, pp. 21–37.

[117] "OpenNap: Open Source Napster Server," August 2007. [Online]. Available: http://opennap.sourceforge.net

[118] P. Francis, "Yoid: Extending the internet multicast architecture," 2000. [Online]. Available: http://www.icir.org/yoid/docs/yoidArch.ps

[119] R. Matei, A. Iamnitchi, and P. Foster, "Mapping the gnutella network," *IEEE Internet Computing*, vol. 6, pp. 50–57, January/February 2002.

[120] C. Schmidt and M. Parashar, "Flexible information discovery in decentralized distributed systems," in *12th IEEE International Symposium on High Performance Distributed Computing (HPDC-12 '03)*. IEEE Computer Science, 2003, p. 226.

[121] K. Sethom, H. Afifi, and G. Pujolle, "Palma: A P2P based Architecture for Location Management," in *7th IFIP International Conference on Mobile and Wireless Communication Networks*. Centre for Telecommunications Research, King's College London, September 2005.

[122] K. Sethom, K. Masmoudi, and H. Afifi, "A secure P2P architecture for location management," in *MEM '05: Proceedings of the 6th international conference on Mobile data management*. New York, NY, USA: ACM Press, 2005, pp. 22–26, ayia Napa, Cyprus.

[123] D. Heutelbeck, "Distributed Space Partitionin Trees and their Application in Mobile Computing," Ph.D. dissertation, Open University Hagen, Germany, May 2005.

[124] S. Androutsellis-Theotokis and D. Spinellis, "A survey of peer-to-peer content distribution technologies," *ACM Comput. Surv.*, vol. 36, no. 4, pp. 335–371, 2004.

[125] Q. Lv, P. Cao, E. Cohen, K. Li, and S. Shenker, "Search and replication in unstructured peer-to-peer networks," in *International Conference on Supercomputing (ICS'02)*. New York, NY, USA: ACM, June 22-26 2002.

[126] B. Y. Zhao, L. Huang, J. Stribling, S. C. Rhea, A. D. Joseph, and J. D. Kubiatowicz, "Tapestry: a resilient global-scale overlay for service deployment," *IEEE Journal on Selected Areas in Communications*, vol. 22, no. 1, pp. 41–53, January 2004. [Online]. Available: http://ieeexplore.ieee.org/xpl/freeabs_all.jsp?arnumber=1258114

[127] S. Rhea, P. Eaton, D. Geels, H. Weatherspoon, B. Zhao, and J. Kubiatowicz, "Pond: The oceanstore prototype," in *FAST '03: Proceedings of the 2nd USENIX Conference on File and Storage Technologies*. Berkeley, CA, USA: USENIX Association, 2003, pp. 1–14.

[128] National Oceanic and Atmospheric Administration, "Report of the Superintendent," United States Coast Survey, Washington, USA, Annual Report 12, June 1877.

[129] Maplesoft, "Maple: The essential tool for mathematics and modeling," January 2009. [Online]. Available: http://www.maplesoft.com/products/Maple/index.aspx

[130] I. Wolfram Research, "Wolfram mathematica 7," January 2009. [Online]. Available: http://www.wolfram.com/products/mathematica/index.html

[131] E. W. Weisstein, "Elliptic intergral," MathWorld - A Wolfram Web Resource, January 2009. [Online]. Available: http://mathworld.wolfram.com/EllipticIntegral.html

[132] B. B. Mandelbrot, *The Fractal Geometry of Nature*. New York, NY, USA: W.H. Freeman and Company, 1983.

List of Acronyms and Symbols

2D	Two-dimensional
3D	Three-dimensional
ACR	Active-Content Replication
ACID	Atomicity, Consistency, Isolation, Durability
CAN	Content Addressable Network
CBS	Context-based System
DFA	Deterministic Finite Automaton
DHT	Distributed Hash Table
DDNS	Dynamic Domain Name System
DSL	Digital Subscriber Line
DSPT	Distributed Space Partitioning Tree
GPS	Global Positioning System
ID	Identifier
IDS	Intrusion Detection System
IP	Internet Protocol
IRC	Internet Relay Chat
LBS	Location-based Service
MER	Mean Error Rate
OLAP	On-Line Analytical Processing
POI	Point of Interest
P2P	Peer-to-Peer
RCS	Reference Coordinate System
SFC	Space-filling Curves
SMER	Small-World Mean Error Rate
SPoF	Single Point of Failure
TTL	Time-to-Live
WKEP	Well-known Entry Point

List of Publications and Contributions to Conferences

I. Conferences and Workshops

1. M.Knoll, M. Helling, S. Holzapfel, A. Wacker and T. Weis
   Bootstrapping Peer-to-Peer Systems using IRC
   5th International Workshop on Collaborative Peer-to-Peer Systems (COPS09), Groningen, The Netherlands, June 29th - July 1st, 2009.

2. M. Knoll, H. Abbadi, and T. Weis
   Replication in Peer-to-Peer Systems
   3rd International Workshop on Self-Organizing Systems (IWSOS 2008), Vienna, Austria, December 10-12, 2008.

3. M. Knoll, A. Wacker, G. Schiele, and T. Weis
   Bootstrapping in Peer-to-Peer Systems
   14th International Conference on Parallel and Distributed Systems (ICPADS 2008), Melbourne, Victoria, Australia, December 8-10, 2008.

4. M. Knoll, A. Wacker, G. Schiele, and T. Weis
   Decentralized Bootstrapping in Pervasive Applications
   PerCom WiP at the 5th Annual International Conference on Pervasive Computing and Communcations (PerCom 2007), White Plains, NY, USA, March 19-23, 2007.

5. M. Saternus, M. Knoll, F. Dürr, and T. Weis
   Symstry: Ein P2P-System für Ortsbezogene Anwendungen
   Kommunikation in Verteilten Systemen (KiVS 2007), Bern, Switzerland, February 26 - March 2nd, 2007.

6. A. Heil, M. Knoll, and T. Weis
   The Internet of Things - Context-based Device Federations
   Hawaii International Conference on System Sciences (HICSS-40), Waikoloa, HI, USA, January 3-6, 2007.

7. M. Knoll and T. Weis
   Optimizing Locality for Self-Organizing Context-based Systems
   International Workshop on Self-Organizing Systems (IWSOS 2006), Passau, Germany, September 18-20, 2006.

8. T. Weis, M. Saternus, M. Knoll, A. Brändle, and M. Combetto
   Towards a General Purpose User Interface for Service-oriented Context-aware Applications
   Advanced Visual Interfaces (AVI), Venezia, Italy, May 23-26, 2006.

9. M. Knoll, T. Weis, A. Ulbrich, and A. Brändle
   Scripting your Home
   2nd International Workshop on Location- and Context-Awareness (LoCA 2006) Dublin, Ireland, May 10-11, 2006.

10. T.Weis, M. Handte, M. Knoll, and C. Becker
    Customizable Pervasive Applications
    4th Annual IEEE International Conference on Pervasive Computing and Communcations (PerCom 2006), Pisa, Italy, March 13-17, 2006.

11. A. Wacker, M. Knoll, T. Heiber, and K. Rothermel
    A New Approach for Establishing Pairwise Keys for Securing Wireless Sensor Networks
    3rd ACM Conference on Embedded Networked Sensor Systems (SenSys 2005), San Diego, CA, USA, November 2-4, 2005.

II. Journals

1. C. Becker, F. Dürr, M. Knoll, D. Nicklas, and T. Weis
   Entwicklung Ortsbezogener Anwendungen
   Kruse, Hans G. (ed.): PIK - Praxis der Informationsverarbeitung und Kommunikation. Bd. 29 (2006) 1., K.G. Saur Verlag, Munich, Germany

2. T. Weis, M. Knoll, A. Ulbrich, G. Mühl, and A. Brändle
   Rapid Prototyping for Pervasive Applications
   IEEE Pervasive Computing 6(2): 76-84 (2007)

III. Books

1. M. Knoll
   Das vernetzte Heim: Sicherheit für drahtlose Kleinstgeräte
   Verlag Dr. Müller, ISBN: 978-3-8364-3032-6

Index

Anonymity, 14
Anycast, 27, 119
Autonomy, 14
Avalanche, 117
Azimuthal Projections, 46

Bittorrent, 4, 116, 122
Bootstrapping, 3, 26, 55, 61, 118
Broadcast, 71, 119

Cachelogic, 4
CAN, 115, 128
Cantor, George, 35
Cartography, 41
Chord, 127
Conformality, 45
Conic Projections, 48
Context Server, 5
Coordinate Systems, 28, 40
Cost-Sharing, 13
Cylindrical Projections, 48

DDNS, 58
Decentralization, 12
DSPT, 124
Dynamics, 13

Earth's Shape, 38
Eckert, 48
eDonkey, 4, 122
eMule, 4

Equidistance, 42
Equivalence, 43

Failover, 52
Fass II, 83
Freenet, 19
Freeriding, 116

Generation Model, 15
Geodesics, 44
Geoid, 38
Geometric Coordinates, 30
Georgia Tech Home, 5
Geostry, 2, 20
Geostry ID, 78
Globase.KOM, 123
Gnutella, 4, 14, 16, 18, 27, 121, 122, 126
GPS, 2
Great Circle Paths, 44
Guardian, 62

Hilbert, 82, 134
HP CoolTown, 5

IRC, 64

Join Network, 25, 66

Kazaa, 4, 15, 19

Latitude, 40

LBS, 2, 5, 27
Leaf Set, 21
Leave Network, 25, 67
Lebesgue, 81
Lindenmayer Systems, 36
Lindenmayer, Aristid, 36
Linearization, 34
Locality, 21, 35
Location Association, 32
Location Modeling, 28
Location-based P2P, 75
Location-based Services, 27
Longitude, 40
Loxodromes, 42

Map Distortion, 41
Map Projections, 38
Map Properties, 41
Mealy Machine, 92
Mean Error Rate, 84
Mollweide, 48
Multicast, 27, 119

Napster, 15, 18, 121
Nearest Neighbor Queries, 33
Neighborhood Queries, 93
Neighborhood Set, 21
Netto, Eugen, 35
Nexus, 5
Node ID, 20, 24, 25

OceanStore, 116, 126

P2P, 11
P2P Advantages, 12
P2P Classification, 14, 15
P2P Lookup, 12
P2P Next, 20
P2P Search, 12

Palma Project, 124
PAST, 20, 127
Pastry, 20, 115
Peano, 81
Peano, Giuseppe, 36
Peer Cache, 118
Peer-to-Peer, 11
Peirce Projection, 79, 133
Position Queries, 33, 88
Pseudoconic Projections, 48
Pseudocylindrical Projections, 48

Random Probing, 118
Range Queries, 34
RectNet, 124
Redirection (Hashing), 105
Redirection (Leafset), 105
Region Queries, 90
Related Work, 115
Replication, 6, 49, 99, 125
Replication (Active Content), 126
Replication (Cache-based), 125
Replication (Passive), 125
Replication (Static Scheme), 127
Replication Goals, 101
Replication Scenarios, 110
Replication Transparency, 52
Routing, 23
Runtime (Routing), 24

S-shaped Curve, 81
Scalability, 13
SCRIBE, 20
Self-Healing, 67
Self-Organization, 12
Servant, 11
Servlet, 16
SFC, 34, 35, 80

Index

SHA-1, 18
Small Worlds, 85
Spatial Queries, 33, 75, 123, 134
SplitStream, 20
Symbolic Coordinates, 29

Tapestry, 126
Tissot Indicatrices, 46
Turtle Graphic, 37

Universal Ring, 120

Watchdog, 62
World Partitioning, 76

Yenta, 119

Zone Indexing, 78

Die VDM Verlagsservicegesellschaft sucht für wissenschaftliche Verlage abgeschlossene und herausragende

Dissertationen, Habilitationen, Diplomarbeiten, Master Theses, Magisterarbeiten usw.

für die kostenlose Publikation als Fachbuch.

Sie verfügen über eine Arbeit, die hohen inhaltlichen und formalen Ansprüchen genügt, und haben Interesse an einer honorarvergüteten Publikation?

Dann senden Sie bitte erste Informationen über sich und Ihre Arbeit per Email an *info@vdm-vsg.de*.

Sie erhalten kurzfristig unser Feedback!

VDM Verlagsservicegesellschaft mbH
Dudweiler Landstr. 99   Telefon +49 681 3720 174
D - 66123 Saarbrücken   Fax   +49 681 3720 1749
www.vdm-vsg.de

Die VDM Verlagsservicegesellschaft mbH vertritt

Printed by Books on Demand GmbH, Norderstedt / Germany